I lick my
cheese

I lick my cheese

AND OTHER REAL NOTES FROM THE ROOMMATE FRONTLINES

By Oonagh O'Hagan

Abrams Image
New York

www.roommatesanonymous.com

Editor: David Cashion
Production Manager: Jacqueline Poirier
Cover design by Galen Smith & Liam Flanagan

First published in another form by Sphere, an imprint of Little, Brown Book Group in Great Britain in 2007

Library of Congress Cataloging-in-Publication Data

O'Hagan, Oonagh.
I lick my cheese : and other real notes from the roommate front-lines / by Oonagh O'Hagan.
p. cm.
ISBN 978-0-8109-8362-5
1. Roommates—Humor. 2. Complaint letters—Humor. I. Title.
PN6231.R62O64 2009
816'.54—dc22
2008030525

Printed and bound in China
10 9 8 7 6 5 4 3 2

HNA
harry n. abrams, inc.
a subsidiary of La Martinière Groupe
115 West 18th Street
New York, NY 10011
www.hnabooks.com

To all those who have endured
not-completely-optional co-habitation

Contents

Foreword

Most of us at some time in our lives will share an apartment or house with somebody we don't know as well as we think—perhaps as a student, leaving home for the first time, or maybe after coming out of a long relationship. It's a fact of modern life—a rite of passage even. If you have shared a place with strangers or, more usually, friends, you will recognize the pattern: people you think are perfectly normal can quickly turn out to be completely insane. Weird habits, idiosyncracies, and obsessions begin to emerge, such as a preoccupation with food labeling or an overzealous use of bleach. And then the notes start to appear.

These little notes range from the tedious to the ridiculous, the amusing to the downright disturbing. Each day can reveal a new issue or problem—and a new note.

I'm fascinated by people's patterns of behavior, and as a graphic designer, I'm particularly intrigued by *the way* they express feelings and beliefs. A note can tell you so much about a person—from the choice of paper, to the words underlined or put in capitals, to the drawings and doodles that illustrate their requests, demands, and complaints. The notes capture everything from lunacy to genius.

Over the years a number of my own roommates have resorted without embarrassment to the written word. One in particular seemed to communicate solely via notes. These notes became increasingly frequent and terrifying, soon escalating into a full-blown catfight—but one that was never openly discussed or even acknowledged. Small talk and general niceties were still exchanged in an apparently natural manner as we passed each other in the hall, but this was the same woman who frantically wrote on the back of a microwave-meal box:

Please don't soak my stuff that's made out of wood—it bends and cracks them when the fibers get full of water. Cheers!

How to react to this? How to feel anything other than utterly baffled, if not unsettled?

As these silent brawls continued between us, ranging from the amount of space my food took up in the fridge to a mythological vendetta against a boyfriend of hers I had never met, I realized we were not alone in this note writing. Soon friends and acquaintances were telling me about ongoing fights involving messages such as:

Someone has eaten my pasta, I'm hungry.

and,

Out of my thirty multivitamins and iron tablets I have only had approximately fifteen. Unless you want to be blamed for me becoming anemic I suggest that whoever has been taking them replace them.

Everyone seemed to be in the midst of either being accused or accusing others of thieving shampoo, squatting in cupboard space, *deliberately* clogging up toilets, and other such weirdness.

As I researched further, I realized the most alarming and irritating were not the aggressive, accusing notes, but the instructive, even enthusiastic ones. I include within this category the roommate who always left out cake and asked for comments on how to make it "even more yummy." If that wasn't nauseating enough, there was the friend's roommate who instead of writing notes just left photocopied extracts from the Bible around the house. And as for the shocking number of people who resort to *typing* their words of wisdom . . .

What does this all mean?

When you start to look into it, *everything* gets discussed through these notes. Love, anger, jealousy, food, hatred—they all feature. And not only is the subject matter random and strange, but so are the items that are written on: the back of a bill, in the margarine and, worst of all, on the walls in snot. But the one thing that links all the writers is the need to be heard without confrontation.

I started to collect these notes. As I did, I realized that not only was this a way to get inside and snoop around people's homes, but it was a fascinating and intriguing way of getting inside their minds. Suddenly a book was emerging, one with secrets, fights, and scandals, but all based on actual people and events. In some instances this book champions those who just want the decent thing done, but I cannot deny that at times it is also a work of revenge. After all those years of torment and torture inflicted by the range of freaks, frumps, and sometimes friends we've had to share our personal space with, here was a chance to fight back. But the note writers should not be too upset; after all, it is also a celebration of their work.

From the mundane to the ridiculous, these messages probably say more about the way we share our lives and relate to other people than a whole library of psychology studies. Behind a few words, scribbled in frustration, rage, desperation, and occasionally goodwill, lies a whole story. You could be pretentious and claim they're almost like poetry, or you could just say they're very, very funny and a little bit disturbing. Either way, I hope you enjoy reading them as much as I enjoyed collecting them. I should point out that not only did I receive the actual notes, but often some (dodgy quality) photos of them—so be forewarned about some of the amateur photography in the book. If you feel that you have a note that is worthy of scrutiny, you can submit it to and keep up-to-date with all new notes on: www.roommatesanonymous.com.

Oonagh

PS. It's not often you get an e-mail asking if it would be OK to have your ass changed. I have tried to keep it under wraps (not my ass) the fact that I am a Brit. Alas, now and again, it would slip out and it popped out over my ass. This is getting a bit confusing. I should explain. There were times where bits in the book had to be changed from my mealy mouthed Brit-speak into more American-friendly lingo. My "arse" therefore had to change into an "ass"; a "flat" or two was converted into "apartments"; and some "pants" turned into your "underwear" while crossing the Atlantic. I hope that makes some sort of sense, as much as anything British makes sense. Jellied eels: need I say more?

"I pay the rent. What do you do?"

PARTIES, LIVING TOGETHER, AND
OTHER NOTES FROM THE LIVING ROOM

The living room is a common room: a communal space full of people with nothing in common. Different creeds and cultures reluctantly come together over a soap or a TV dinner. TV is often the main hub of a living room but, unlike the edited "reality" on TV, here all the fights are real and there is no off switch when you get sick of the puerile arguments.

My favorite notes come from situations in which the living room has slowly morphed into another room, usually a bedroom, and becomes the scene of embarrassing entwinements, boyfriends slowly becoming permanent fixtures on couches, and other behavior that should be reserved for rooms with locks. Talking of locks, when a living room starts being the popular venue for any type of personal grooming (see note on toenail clippings), you know that you have the potential catalyst for a "roommate meeting." Sadly, it is difficult to take a roommate meeting at all seriously. Very rarely have I heard of this kind of organized discussion working well. In fact, the only time it seems to work is when interrogating—sorry, *interviewing*—potential new roommates; fresh meat to dissect and prod, this appears to be the one thing that can bring an otherwise fraught and disjointed household together.

I hang my head in shame even thinking about roommate interviewing, as I have found myself part of these character assassinations. It is horribly entertaining to watch your victim squirm as they attempt to sell themselves to you. There are some people you know you are not going to get on with almost immediately. It can be their smile, handshake, or cheesy wink, but more often it is their hobbies that are the clinchers for straight rejection. I have personally rejected a perfectly nice young gentleman from New Zealand. I wasn't totally impressed with his answers or aesthetics (shallow but true—if you are going to see them every day it is an added bonus if they are easy on the eye) but everything seemed to be going decently until he said that what he had really been looking for was somewhere with a huge dick. He continued through the noise of our all-female household's jaws hitting the floor, telling us that there was nothing like a big dick and sunshine to make sure you slept well. It was only when he said that he could see why there weren't many big dicks in London to *lie on* that the penny dropped. Lie on? Where were these amazing creatures that you could lie on? Oh God, he means *deck*, a deck, oh, thank God, a deck, a sundeck. Our Kiwi gentleman looked baffled about why two potential roommates had hurried out of the living room with wry smiles followed by muffled laughter. I was left to show our deck lover the door, explaining to him we would have a think and let him know once we had interviewed everyone who was interested in the room. I also pointed out that I too was disappointed that we didn't have a big dick in the apartment.

Curiously, it is when the interrogators shift to being the interrogated that another roommate-bonding moment occurs. As potential new recruits ask how much the bills are or comment that the facilities aren't very good, it is difficult not to become defensive of your humble communal areas. How dare a complete stranger turn his or her snooty nose up at your living space? The area you have despised and the people you have bitched about suddenly become your domain and your comrades. What is this viewer's problem with the living room? Don't they like the squatter on the couch or the toenail clippings? Don't they want to join our commune? Big decks to them.

THIS PHONE HAS BEEN
UP MY ASS !!

This note came from a woman who had been away from her apartment for a few days and whose parents were visiting the next afternoon. Upon her arrival home, she walked in to find, judging from the general disarray, that a very successful party had recently ended. She also discovered that in the kitchen was an unknown gentleman in a suit, lying face down on the floor. That was not the most disturbing part of it. The phone lying next to him had a Post-it note on it that read: "This phone has been up my ass." Eventually she and the roommates who were the culprits for the party managed to clean the whole apartment and the visiting parents were none the wiser. The only evidence that anything ever happened that night is the note. She has since bought a new phone.

Dear [illegible]

You will be glad to know that my grandfather's visit to Edinburgh was a success. Not only did he manage to get to the top of our stairs alive, but when he did so & settled into our sofa with a cup of tea, he was enlivened by the sight of your 2 foot long bong which you had thoughtfully left on display on the coffee table.

I shall remember to be as equally as thoughtful upon your next grand-parental visit.

[illegible]

The recipient of this note sounds like he could possibly, maybe, perhaps be a smoker of marijuana. Of course, I might be totally wrong, and I am by no means saying someone like this person would ever have inhaled. I do in fact understand that he had actually cleaned up the apartment (even leaving out some fancy tea), but somehow had managed not to notice his favorite memento from Morocco . . .

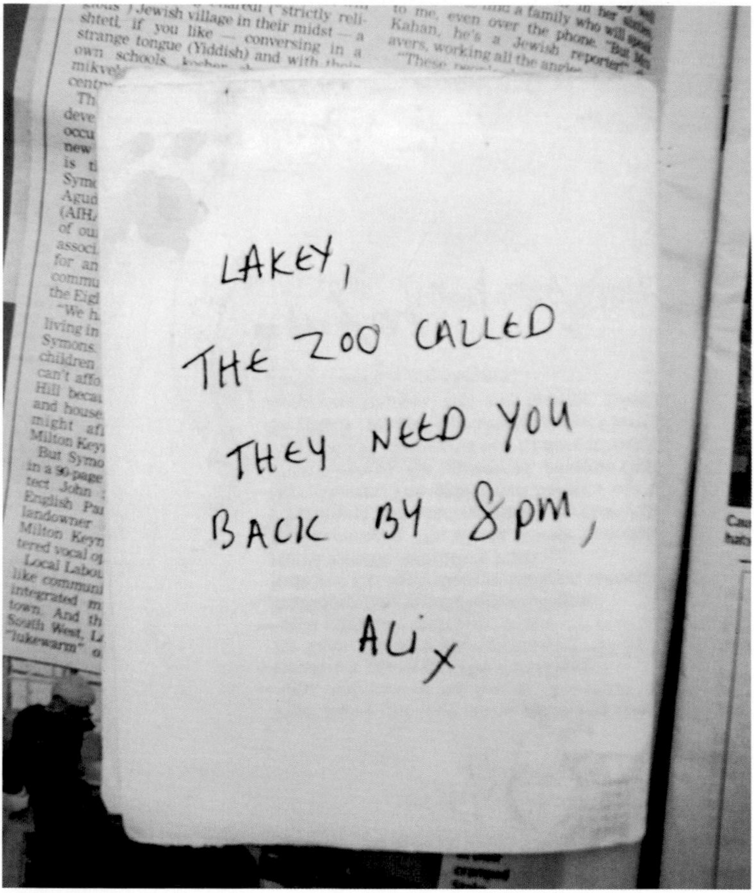
LAKEY,
THE ZOO CALLED
THEY NEED YOU
BACK BY 8pm,
ALi x

Subtle yet effective.

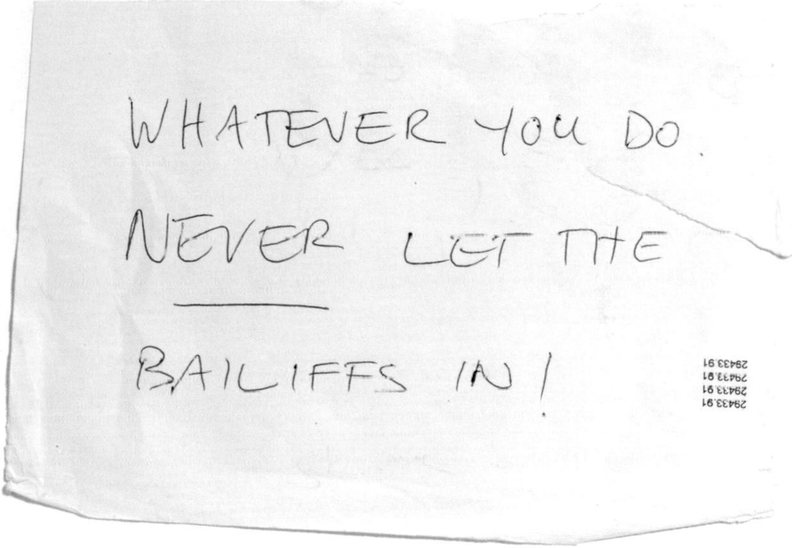
WHATEVER YOU DO
NEVER LET THE
BAILIFFS IN!

Ah. Now this sounds familiar. I had a "bailiff incident" once. I had been writing checks for the bills to another roommate. Little did I realize that the roommate was spending the money on a mixture of vices. The first I knew of this was when the doorbell rang and the bailiffs were at the door. Knowing how these things work, I realized that if I let them in they would take anything that wasn't bolted down. The roommate who had misappropriated the money wasn't the brightest bulb, seeing as he thought I wouldn't find out.

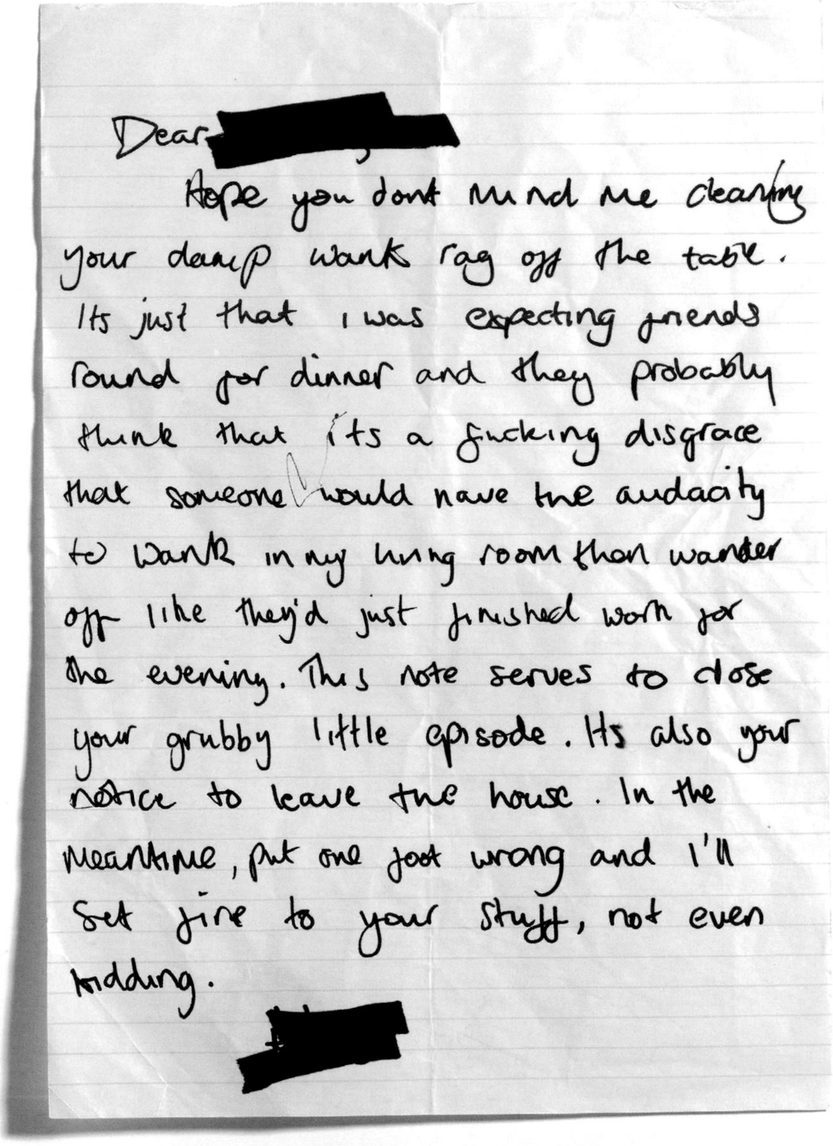

Dear [redacted],

Hope you dont mind me cleaning your damp wank rag off the table. Its just that I was expecting friends round for dinner and they probably think that its a fucking disgrace that someone would have the audacity to wank in my living room then wander off like they'd just finished work for the evening. This note serves to close your grubby little episode. Its also your notice to leave the house. In the meantime, put one foot wrong and I'll set fire to your stuff, not even kidding.

[redacted]

Sometimes the horror of a face-to-face confrontation is totally understandable—and this is one of those situations. This note appears to want to shame this person even further, he possibly not having been shamed enough following the discovery that he'd turned an idle moment into an opportunity to explore solo sexual pleasure . . . in the living room. Pleasuring oneself in the communal area might be OK if people would at least be courteous enough to dispose of the evidence. Worryingly this seems, pardon the awful pun, to come up quite often.

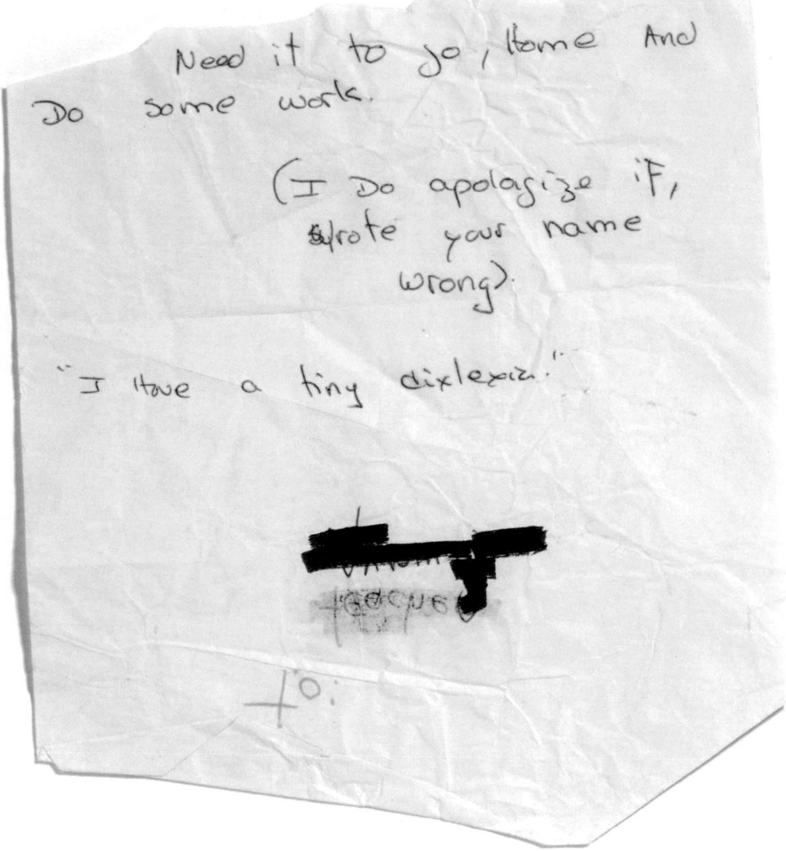

Need it to go, Home And
Do some work.

(I Do apolagize iF,
wrote your name
wrong).

"I Have a tiny dixlexia."

[redacted]

To:

Living with someone whose first language is not yours is not easy. Living with someone whose first language is not yours and has dyslexia can be a *real* challenge. It is difficult enough to decide whether you should point out grammatical errors without the added element of them being foreign and their sole reason for living in the country being to learn the language, but you can get into a serious minefield if you start thinking they have difficulties in their own language as well as their second. In any case, this person seems to have recognized that they need to go home and do some work. And at least they just have "a tiny dixlexia" and not a tiny something else. Hopefully.

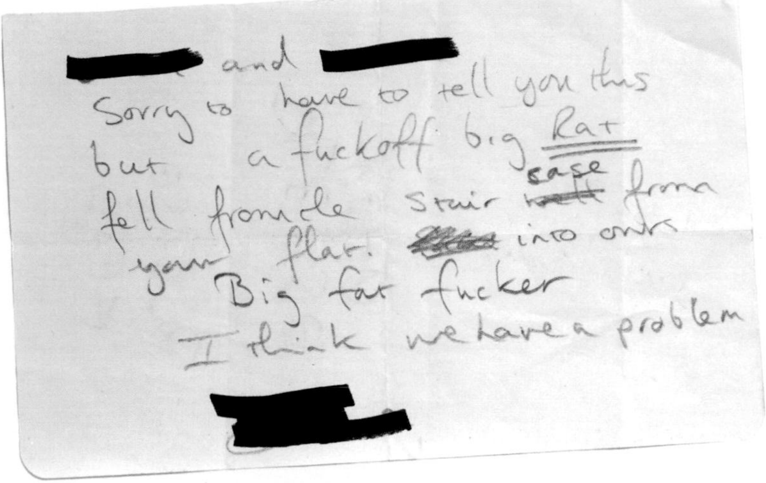

[redacted] and [redacted]
Sorry to have to tell you this
but a fuckoff big Rat
fell from de Stair ~~well~~ case from
your flat! ~~[illegible]~~ into ours
Big fat fucker
I think we have a problem

[redacted]

They're watching you, they're around every corner. Yes, rodents and other pests. According to that center of all useless and dubious statistics, the Internet, there are three rats to every one person in some major cities. You thought you only had two roommates . . . maybe you have a few more who are even less sociable.

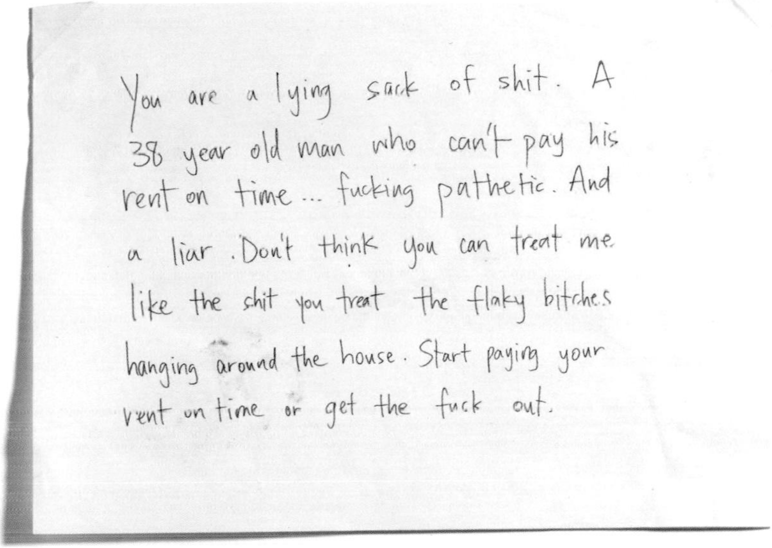

You are a lying sack of shit. A 38 year old man who can't pay his rent on time... fucking pathetic. And a liar. Don't think you can treat me like the shit you treat the flaky bitches hanging around the house. Start paying your rent on time or get the fuck out.

I'm sensing anger . . .

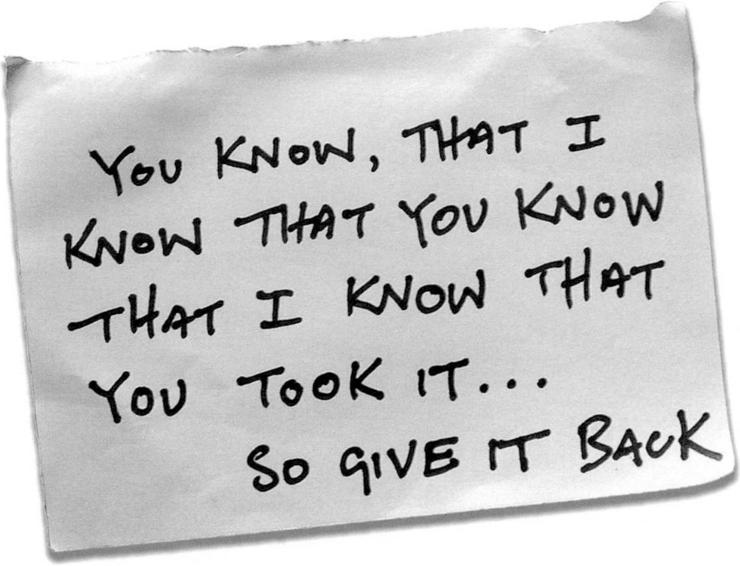
YOU KNOW, THAT I
KNOW THAT YOU KNOW
THAT I KNOW THAT
YOU TOOK IT...
SO GIVE IT BACK

The fact that the "it" goes undefined makes this note terrifying. It's all smoke and mirrors, winks and nods. This is the kind of message that the mafia would leave for a victim as the first chance to pay up before getting to wear the not-so-fashionable concrete shoes.

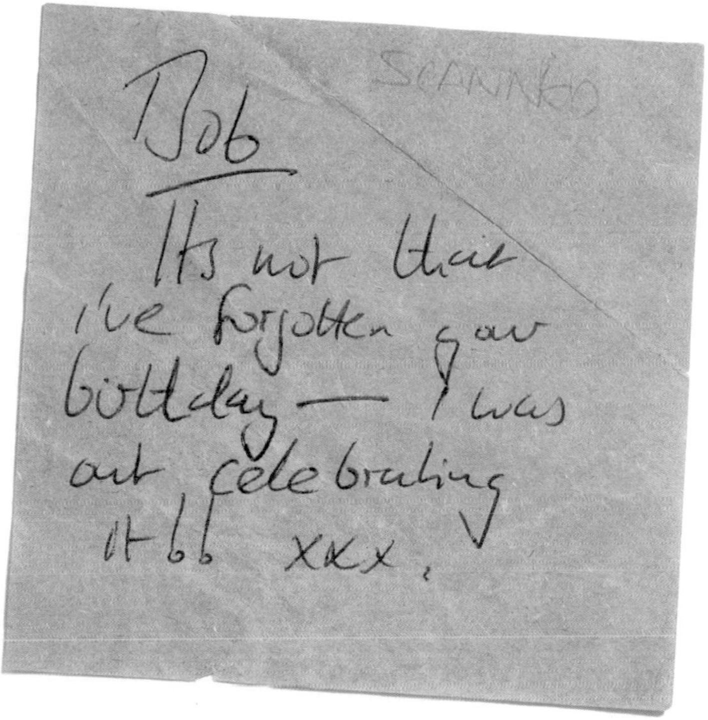
SCANNED
Bob
Its not that
i've forgotten your
birthday — I was
out celebrating
it!! xxx.

You can't help liking this character, a bit of a lovable rogue. Apologizing, but having far too good a time to ever really be sorry. Bless.

oo est la Kirsty Allsopp ?
BLADE
BO' SELECTA! 2
Serpico

("Where is Kirsty"). . . when you need her? Is this a last-gasp attempt to find yourself somewhere else to stay? Has Kirsty become the patron saint of roommates? Where are you, blessed Kirsty?

2ND
2ND
Here's a
stamp.
Write to your
mum.
She keeps
calling

Moms everywhere, we feel your pain. The world is divided into those who phone their moms and those who don't. I know a guy who used to phone his mom once, sometimes twice a day, ending with "I love you so much." Jesus.

CONGRATULATIONS!
WE KNEW YOU COULD DO IT !!
V.G well done.

When sharing a space works out, it can be great. You have an extended social circle, even an extended family. How nice to have everyone rooting for you.

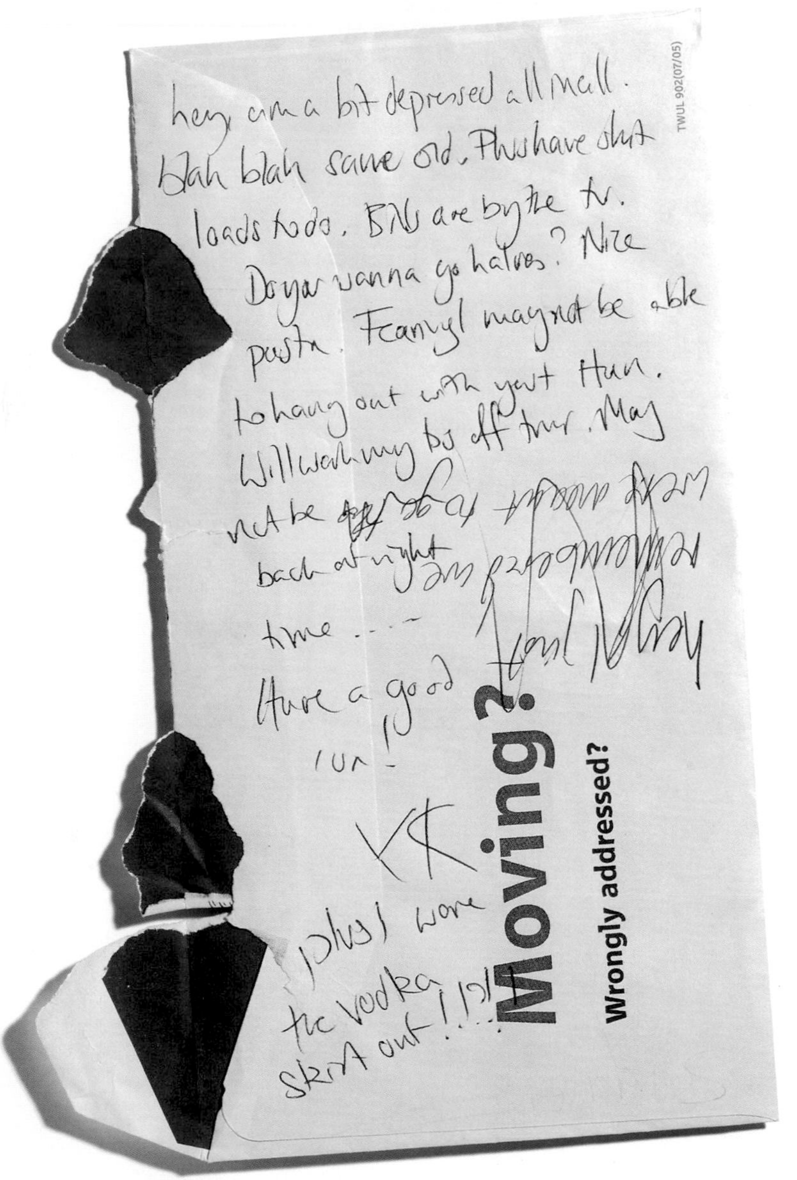
TWUL 902(07/05)
Moving?
Wrongly addressed?
blah blah same old.
Do you wanna go halves?
back at night
time....
Have a good
run!
the vodka

This note initially could be overlooked, as it is the PS that is the main point. The vodka skirt? I did some research into this one. Apparently the "vodka skirt" was bought under the influence. In the cold light of day it was a rather garish garment, so wearing the vodka skirt was seen as the start of a seriously kamikaze night out.

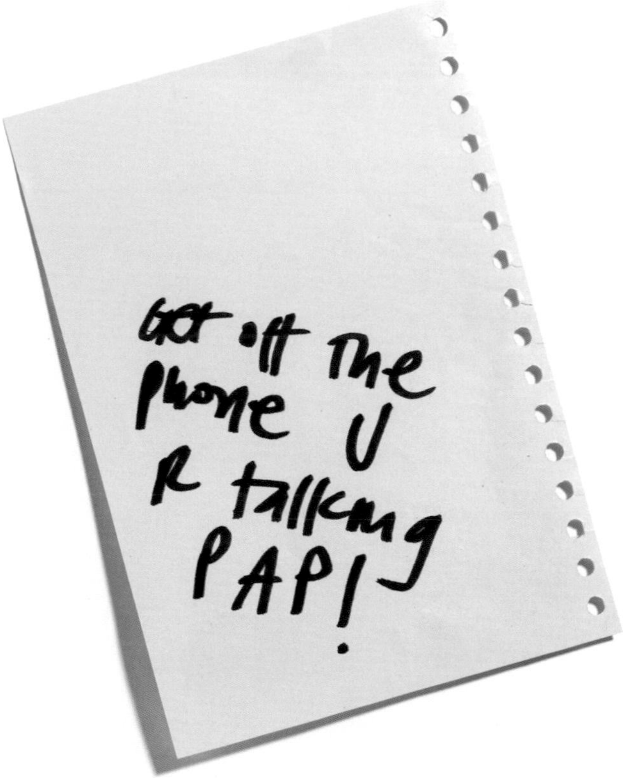
Get off the phone U R talking PAP!

We are essentially selfish creatures and, let's face it, most of us think what we say is much more important than what anyone else says. It is always other people that talk "pap" on the phone. So yeah, get the hell off the phone! Though who says "pap?" Maybe this lot should be disconnected.

Big Surprise!
The rent But
in my
account!!!!!!

Rent. Often the root of all evil in apartment sharing. The strange thing is, there is always one person in the apartment who understands that paying the rent is a condition of living there and another for whom the connection is not so clear. The result is that the former organizes everything for the latter which, similarly to the cleaning-obsessive scenario (see bathroom section), suits the lazy rent-dodging bastard of a roommate just fine.

Well I spoke to none other
than Ringo Starr (!) - the very
comfortingly ran me through
various procedures & eventually
I was connected! (via the yellow cable)
It was rather overwhelming
that he calmly knew so much!
I was too grateful to bother
him about anything else.
I have tomor afternoon off so
will do some rooter research!

B.

I love this note because, once you understand the background, it actually makes sense. But until then it sounds totally bonkers. The call was to an Internet helpline, and the man on the end of the line was named Mr. Starr. His nickname had obviously become "Ringo"—thus the comments about him knowing his stuff and yellow cable. It is not a euphemism for anything else.

I've got popcorn in my pants
—Jess

Having a party in your pants? Has this person been scarfing up the popcorn so ferociously that it has gotten into all their crevices? If this is how they fumble with their popcorn, repeatedly missing the mouth with such a violent trajectory, I would give them a wide berth. Any other encounters could leave you with an injury.

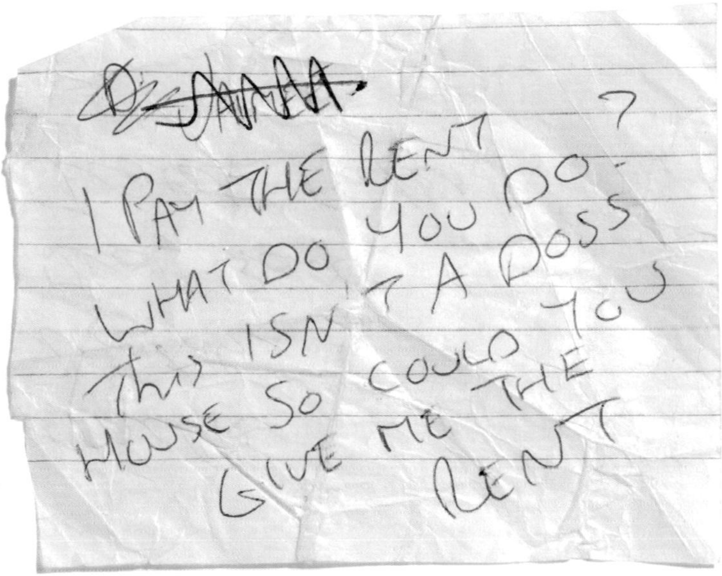
I PAY THE RENT
WHAT DO YOU DO?
THIS ISN'T A DOSS
HOUSE SO COULD YOU
GIVE ME THE
RENT

Simply existing can be pretty difficult in these cut-throat times, but even more so when you seem to be a host to a parasite. This is one of those moments when if you were requested to fill in a form asking you if you had any dependants, you would be inclined to say, "Yes, all my roommates."

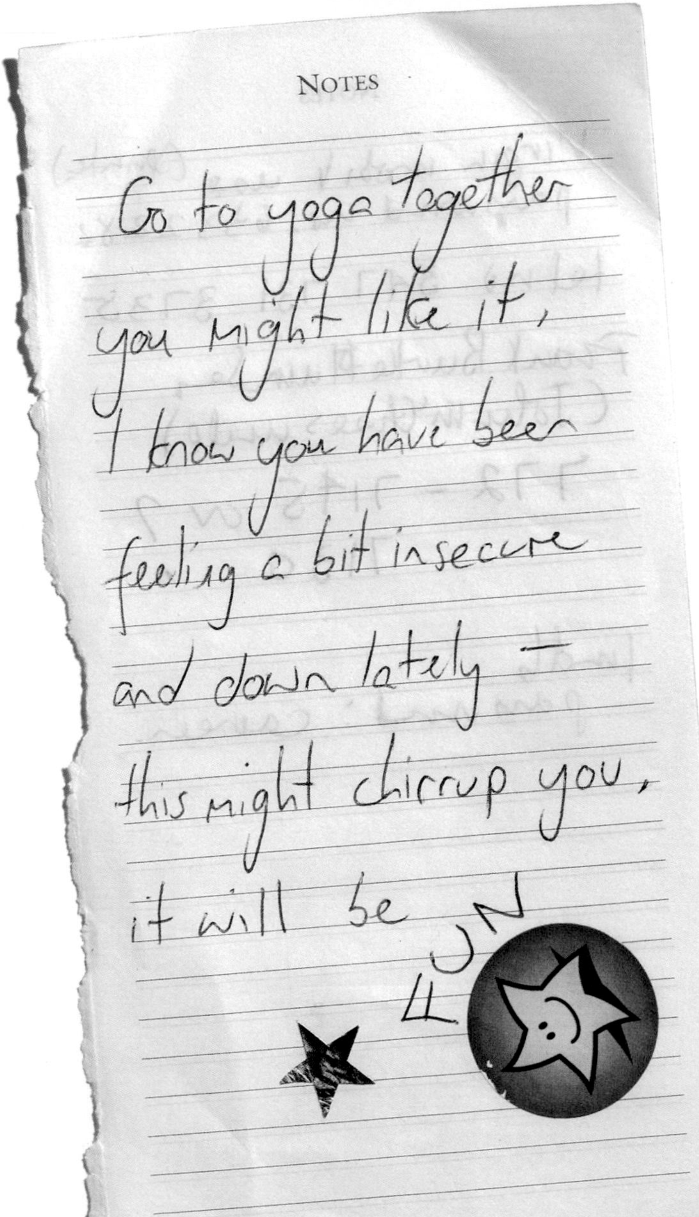

NOTES

Go to yoga together
you might like it,
I know you have been
feeling a bit insecure
and down lately —
this might chirrup you,
it will be FUN

Well-meaning, but I can't help wondering whether the person who received this note really wanted to be reminded, as they walked into their apartment after a hard day, that everybody knew they'd been "feeling a bit insecure and down lately."

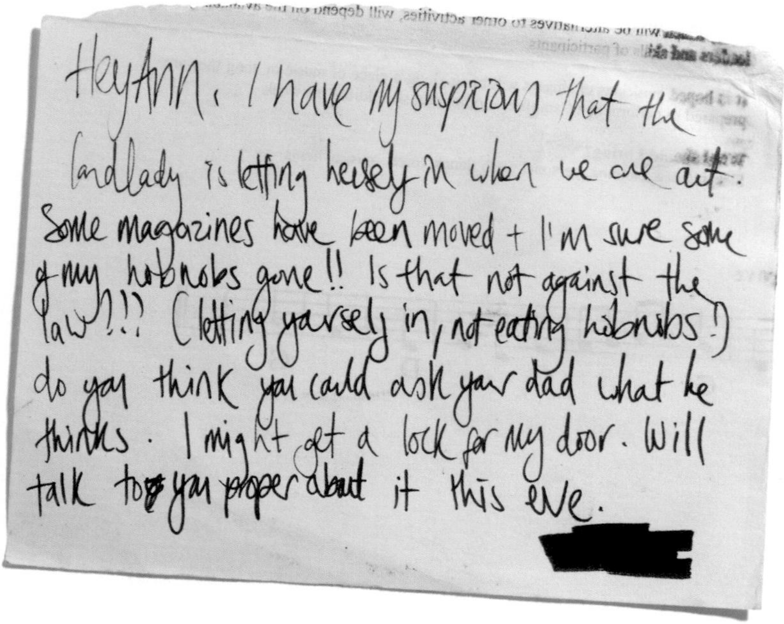
Hey Ann. I have my suspicions that the
landlady is letting herself in when we are out.
Some magazines have been moved + I'm sure some
of my hobnobs gone!! Is that not against the
law?!? (letting yourself in, not eating hobnobs!)
do you think you could ask your dad what he
thinks. I might get a lock for my door. Will
talk to you proper about it this eve.
[redacted]

Once a landlord starts this kind of behaviour, they can become nonchalant. They start by letting themselves into the apartment. No one notices, so they move on to slipping in and having a quick read of the magazines. Again, nobody notices. Before you know it, they're having baths and eating your cookies while wearing your underwear. I don't know if the landlady really was letting herself in. There are lots of urban myths about tenants discovering spy cameras behind mirrors but I have never heard any about cookie thieves. It should definitely be illegal, though—HobNobs, in particular, are great.

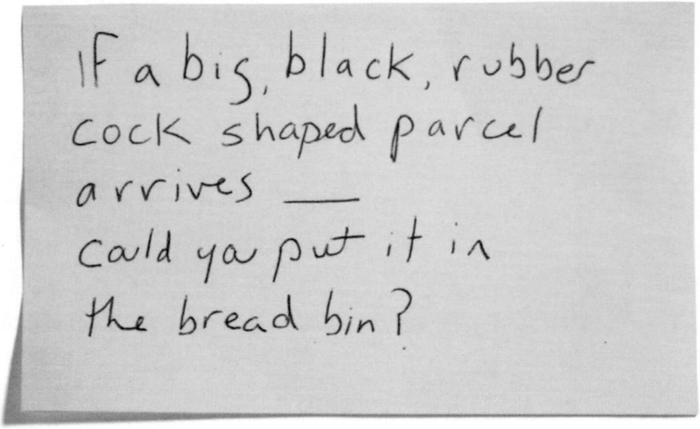
If a big, black, rubber
cock shaped parcel
arrives —
could you put it in
the bread bin?

Where are the days that even mentioning the word "cock" would have caused gasps, never mind getting a big, realistic, rubber one sent right to your front door? It has probably been delivered from a Web site called something like www.jerkcocks.com. In fact, maybe this is the result of someone innocently surfing the net looking for Caribbean chicken recipes and before they know it they had ordered a whole shipment of sex toys. God bless the Internet.

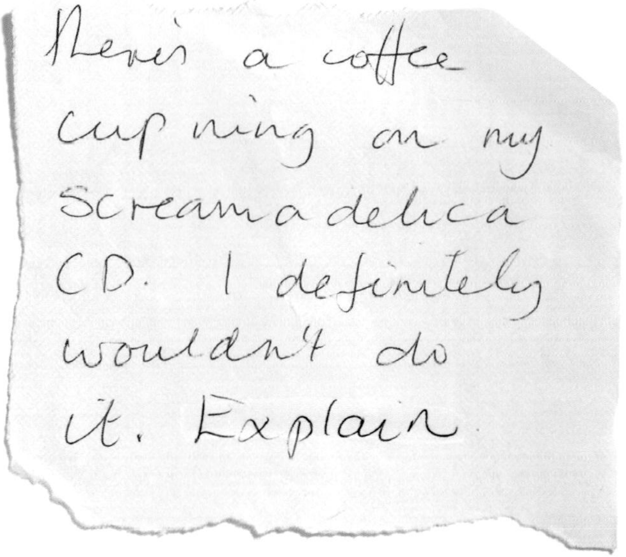
There's a coffee
cup ring on my
Screamadelica
CD. I definitely
wouldn't do
it. Explain

Shiny silver coasters. This is the fate I think all CDs eventually face.

MK14 6DY.
Ask before you borrow my
Stuff!! — my skirt is totally
stretched after you have shoved
it over your Fat Arse. You are
one of the most SELFISH people I
have ever met

There must have been some denial about body shape here. The "stretcher" probably says she is a size ten when she is closer to a size twenty. She once got a single boob into a size-ten boob tube, thus she now claims to be a size ten. I confess to doing this myself (making the claim, not the boob squeeze). But I can't help thinking well of the "stretcher." She didn't care—she just wanted to wear something nice for a night out even if it meant it would be like a long piece of filo pastry by the time she had finished with it.

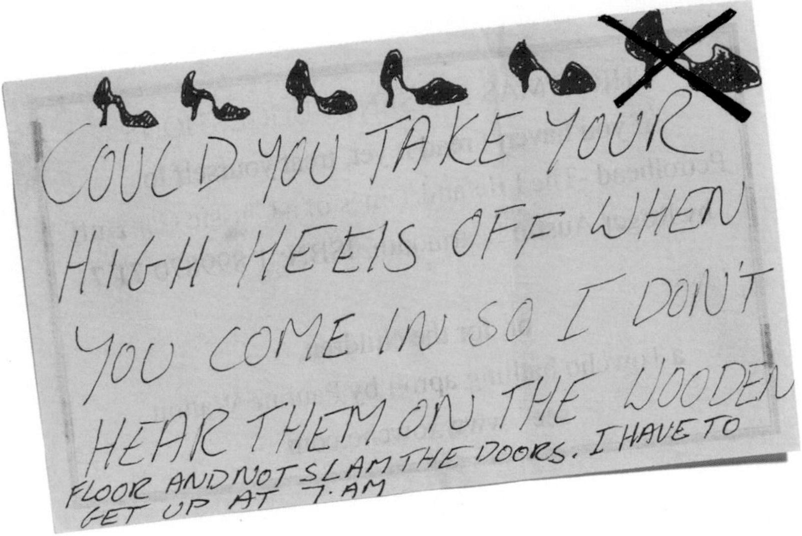
COULD YOU TAKE YOUR
HIGH HEELS OFF WHEN
YOU COME IN SO I DON'T
HEAR THEM ON THE WOODEN
FLOOR AND NOT SLAM THE DOORS. I HAVE TO
GET UP AT 7. AM

One of my friends never recovered from watching a work colleague enter her apartment and walk all over her wooden floor in high heels. One of the tips of the heels had come off, leaving what looked like bullet holes all over the beautifully polished and newly laid floor. (The situation got even worse when she pushed back the sofa to get a better view of the TV and left a deep scar in the wood.)

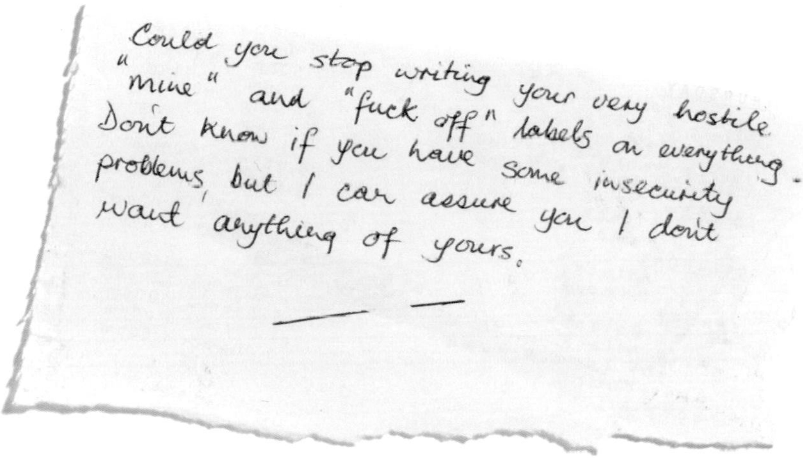
Could you stop writing your very hostile
"mine" and "fuck off" labels on everything.
Don't know if you have some insecurity
problems, but I can assure you I don't
want anything of yours.

Living in several, different shared spaces can leave you emotionally scarred and paranoid. In trying to nip any future problems in the bud, this roommate has been somewhat over-zealous and abusive with labeling their items. Some grocery abuse had obviously taken place in a previous life: garlic assaulted, cereal kidnapped. They are just looking after their property.

HAPPY EASTER
from a
cute chick!

These little yellow chicken things are slightly creepy and this one looks as though it has been hanged from the door. Not so much a celebration of new life as a satanic chicken sacrifice. A nice play on words, though.

House rule:
No nose
Sucking

I just don't think I have any interest in erotic nose play. I might be intrigued if this were a Cyrano de Bergerac or a Pinocchio situation. Maybe then I might find myself thinking, "Well, that is one hell of a nose." But honestly, I just don't see myself saying, "That nose has really got me going, I simply have to have a suck on it." And then draining the dregs of a cold out of somebody's conk? Rather un-sexy. Nope, it's settled, I'm not that into noses.

mosquito

Essentially this is not a note, but I wanted to include it, as it speaks volumes. Waking up to find that your body has been treated like a canteen by hungry mosquitos can be very alarming. However, mosquitoes wouldn't have been the first pests to spring to my mind as being a bane to residents of apartments—I would have thought mice are public enemy numero uno. Such clever rodents: when you do actually catch them, you realize how small, harmless, and cute they are. You forget how many of their droppings you have probably eaten in your "fruit and flakes" cereal. Did you really think the cereal companies had just felt a bit more generous and put more raisins in your muesli? Hell no. Look at the tiny gnaw marks on your packet and you will realize you have been wading your way through oats and mouse poo. Ah well, it's all fiber. But back to the tiny insect bloodsuckers—when they get in at night you can understand someone's glee at killing them. It's not quite a stag's head on a wall, but a mosquito on a piece of card is still a very satisfactory kill and is the one example of hunting I can sympathize with.

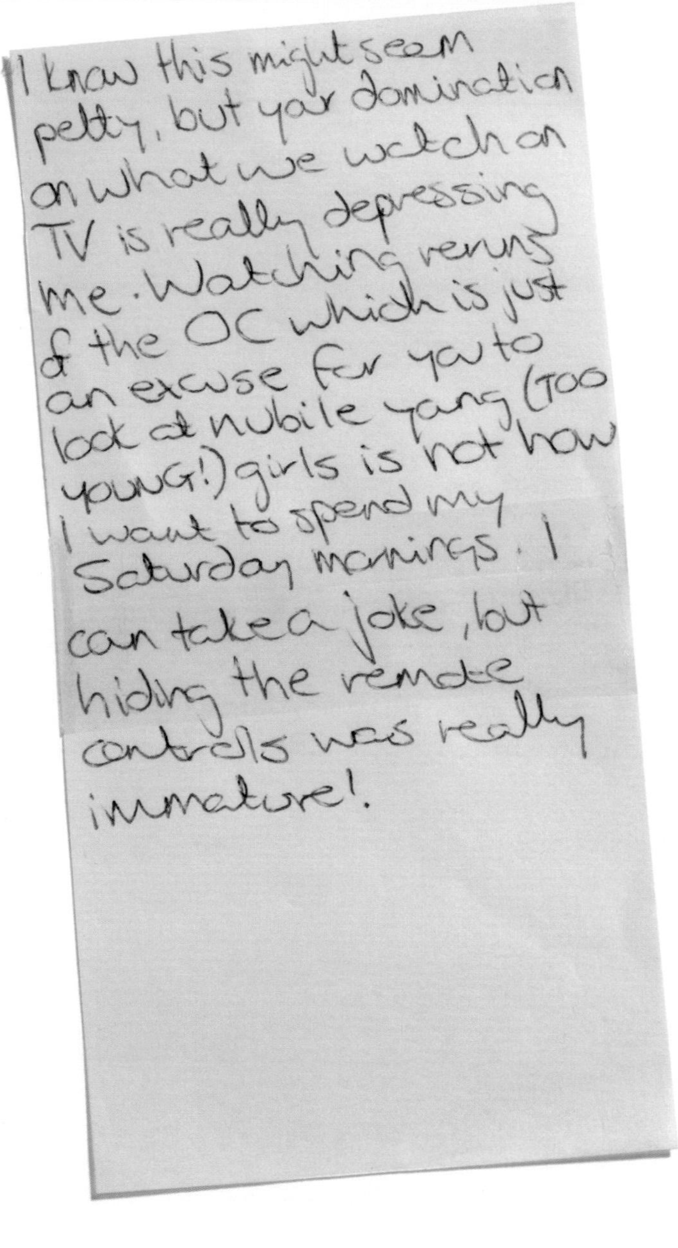

I know this might seem
petty, but your domination
on what we watch on
TV is really depressing
me. Watching reruns
of the OC which is just
an excuse for you to
look at nubile young (TOO
YOUNG!) girls is not how
I want to spend my
Saturday mornings. I
can take a joke, but
hiding the remote
controls was really
immature!

Immature, but probably very funny. As a female, I find many programs on TV pretty depressing, but at least they make some vague attempt at having a storyline. Some other countries seem to have nothing but beauty contests (interestingly only the bikini round) on every channel all the time. OK, so the last thing you want to see in the morning is someone half your age with skin so taut you could bounce quarters off her belly, but the key to living together is compromise. If you can't compromise, get rid of the cable channels and take the batteries out of the remote.

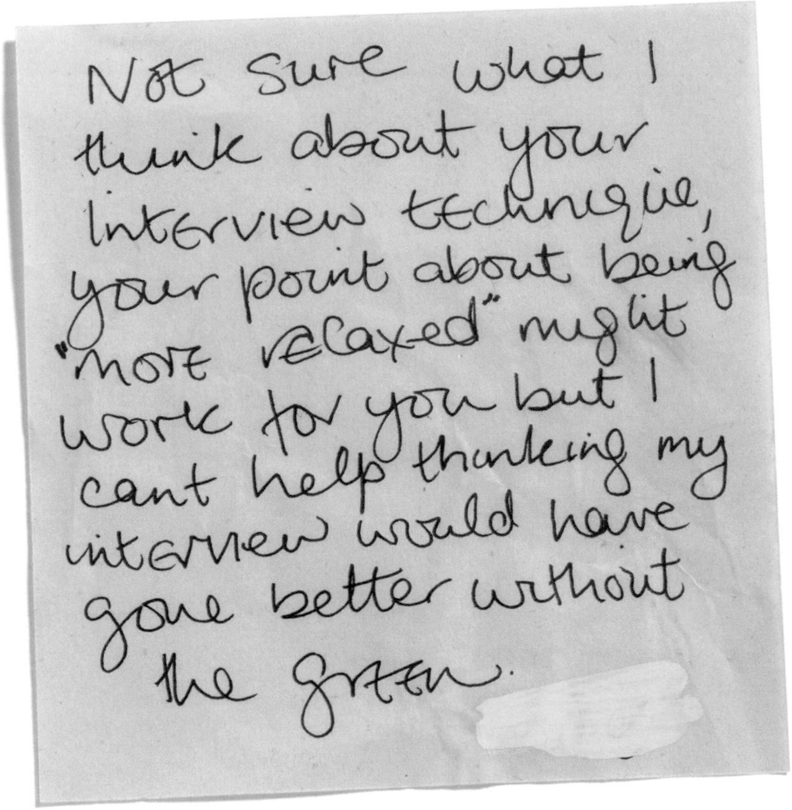
Not sure what I
think about your
interview technique,
your point about being
"more relaxed" might
work for you but I
cant help thinking my
interview would have
gone better without
the green.

This note shows the lengths some individuals will go to calm their nerves and contains the clear lesson never to listen to anyone else's advice. Going to an interview drunk or, as with this character, drugged ("green" being marijuana for those pretending not to know), I wouldn't have thought is the best start. The fact that the interviewee listened to this clown and actually "smoked the green" does not mark him out as the most employable character.

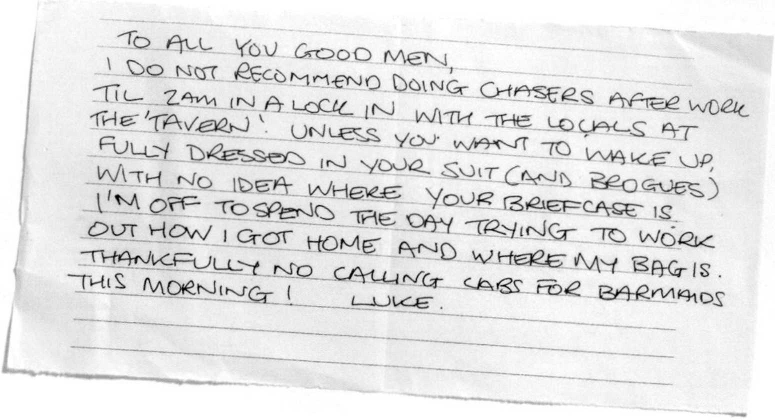

TO ALL YOU GOOD MEN,
I DO NOT RECOMMEND DOING CHASERS AFTER WORK
TIL 2AM IN A LOCK IN WITH THE LOCALS AT
THE 'TAVERN'! UNLESS YOU WANT TO WAKE UP,
FULLY DRESSED IN YOUR SUIT (AND BROGUES)
WITH NO IDEA WHERE YOUR BRIEFCASE IS
I'M OFF TO SPEND THE DAY TRYING TO WORK
OUT HOW I GOT HOME AND WHERE MY BAG IS.
THANKFULLY NO CALLING CABS FOR BARMAIDS
THIS MORNING! LUKE.

This behavior is bad enough when you live on your own—the dark depression of waking up with no idea what you did the night before, but aware that the result feels like a vise squeezing your head. For this individual, it is made a thousand times worse by the fact he has an audience. An audience that, judging by this note, is happy to remind him of the different waifs and strays he has not only socialized with but lured back to his stale room. Luke doesn't get much sympathy seeing as the female is known only as "barmaid"—perhaps she had a lucky escape. And perhaps he should stick to the soft drinks next time.

LUCY
STAY
ALIVE
WE
LOVE
U

As this plea is written in comedy magnetic letters on a refrigerator rather than in a card, I presume that Lucy isn't really close to death. It seems a little too, well, upbeat. But this has given me a fantastic idea. When I die, maybe I could get a metal casket and my family and friends could use these magnets to write all sorts of happy, loving messages on my coffin. On second thought, everyone might get carried away and who knows what they'd end up spelling on me. ("W. H. O. R. . . ") Let's forget that one.

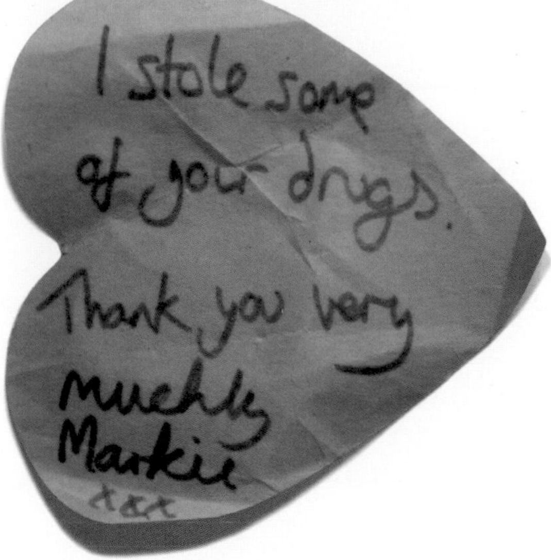
I stole some
of your drugs.
Thank you very
muchly
Markie
x&x

Sheesh! You put your life and street cred on the line by trying to be all cool while striking a deal for whatever drug you desire with some unsavory character. How do you get thanked? By having it stolen from you before you have even had a chance to get high. You didn't even get to make a fool of yourself in some bad nightclub, thinking you are the world's greatest dancer and that you love everyone in the whole sweaty place. Wait a minute—I have had a horrid thought: this isn't like someone's asthma/angina/diabetic drug, is it? Have two lives been put at risk in a crazy attempt to see if insulin gets you high? Oh God, why can't everyone just stay at home with basic cable and drink cocoa?

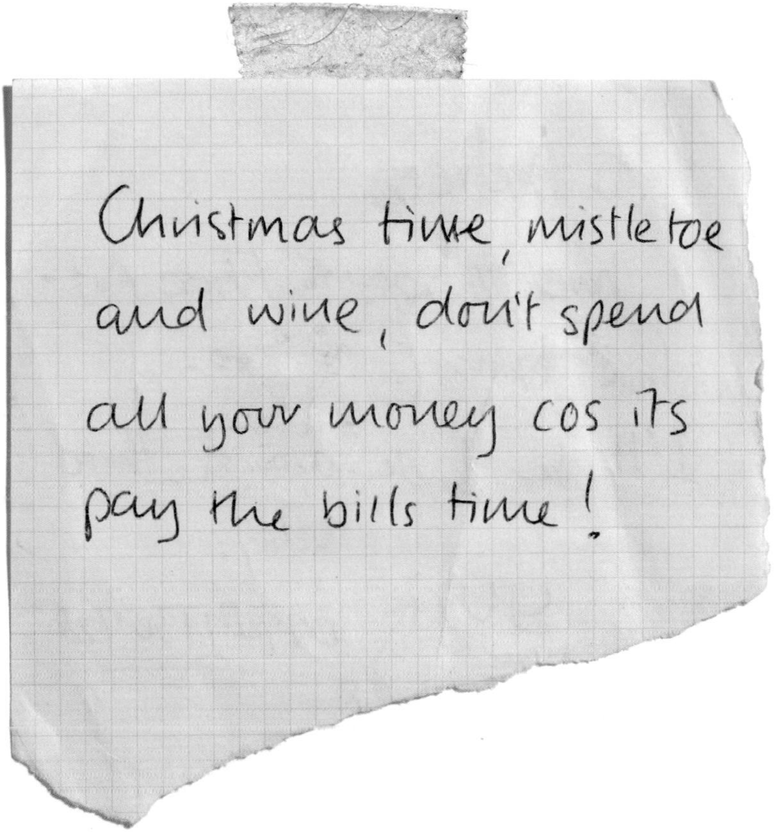
Christmas time, mistletoe and wine, don't spend all your money cos its pay the bills time!

Knowing the lyrics to a cheesy Cliff Richard song is bad enough, but then using it to remind roommates that even at Christmas they still have bills to pay, and therefore can't really go out and enjoy themselves, seems a little harsh.

Can any members of the household lucky enough to be enjoying a sexual ~~relationship~~ erectionship please save your, erm, prophylactic wrappings ... I want to make a dress with them.

Thank you, and enjoy yourselves.

Sapoly!

You know you have hit a sexual low and that your libido has hit a sexual high when you are basing art projects around other people's used condoms. They will probably make millions and we will see it in the Museum of Modern Art next year. Why have I spent my life collecting these roommate notes when I should have been collecting used Trojans? Oh, silly me.

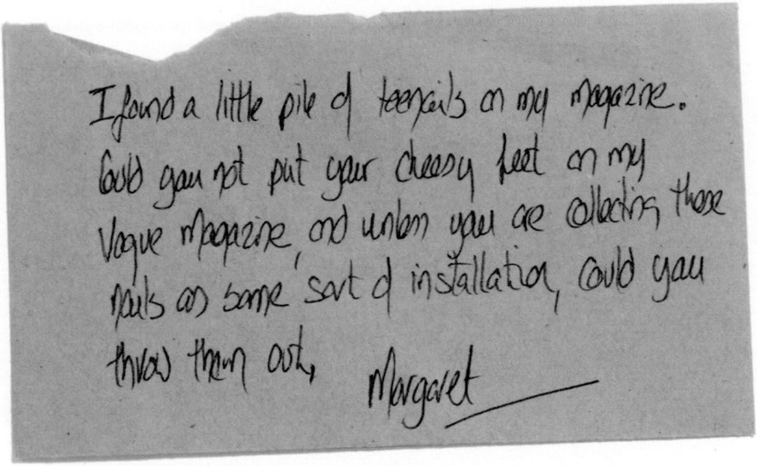

I found a little pile of toenails on my magazine.
Could you not put your cheesy feet on my
Vogue magazine, and unless you are collecting those
nails as some sort of installation, could you
throw them out,
Margaret

How ironic that the fashion bible should be strewn with toenails and smelling of "cheesy feet." The use of the word "installation" in the note leads me to guess the toenail clipper is an artist and for this reason he or she was very aware of the irony of the placement of the clippings and that, yes, this was a piece of art, a commentary on what they thought of fashion—cheesy.

STOP BUTT FLICKING INTO MY GARDEN!!!
YOUR NEIGHBOUR

I had to read this note a few times to get a grip on what was going on. Initially it sounded like some grizzly sex game I had not heard of. I thought there might be groups of people at twilight hanging their rears over garden fences while anonymous neighbors flicked their butts with garden utensils. It quickly became apparent that it was the equally antisocial habit of stubbing out a cigarette only to deposit it in the garden next door. This is often the result of out-of-window illicit smoking—a habit not just reserved for teens experimenting with the evil tobacco weed but of grown adults who, to get accepted into an apartment have lied to the landlord that they are non-smokers. Similar lies are that they won't have people over to stay and they will not play loud music. Yeah, yeah, you lying butt flickers.

Hi lovely, I feel really bad
for -- saying this and
your brother is really lovely and
I know he's at a bit of a
loose end but how long is he
going to be staying in our living
room? It is beginning to get a
bit awkward, and I don't see
him making a big effort to get
a job or find somewhere else
to live. If he could arrange
something for the weekend.
Sorry I know you will understand.

[redacted]

[redacted]

P.S He has eaten quit a
lot of my stuff

[redacted]

I can't help wondering how lovely the brother really was. I had a roommate who had a creepy male friend. I hated it when the friend would come and stay. He wore full cycling gear (ie. tight Lycra) at all times, but there was no sign of a bike. The tightness of the attire made me nervous and he had a slightly musty smell. Altogether there was too much oddness and staring on his part for my liking.

NUFF RESPECT
TO THE
JESUS.
FEEL THE JESUS.
FEEL HIM

This was a Christmas message to the household. It beats "Season's greetings and a Happy New Year."

"You stink like a big fat stinker."

PERSONAL HYGIENE AND
OTHER NOTES FROM THE BATHROOM

According to one of the many weird and wonderful statistics revealed each day in the press, every one of us spends an average of three years on the toilet during our lifetime. Finding solace in the bathroom is nothing new. In different cultures and throughout history there have been long and elaborate rituals and traditions relating to cleaning and hygiene. From the Romans and bathing to the Chinese and massage, huge amounts of time and thought have been put into what I refer to here as "bathroom behavior."

However for some people nowadays, busy lives mean these rituals have been either condensed or completely eradicated from daily routines. The well-being of teeth, skin, and orifices are left in the much cleaner hands of the gods. These individuals waft around blissfully unaware of their odor. The fact is, we all struggle to detect our own smell. Mortifyingly, this is because we are no longer sensitive to it, but, unfortunately, that doesn't apply to the odor of stinking roommates. It takes a brave and/or tactless person to let someone know that every time they speak they are gassing them with their halitosis. At the same time, however, a trip to any local supermarket would reveal rows of shelves featuring an array of products dedicated to cleaning and hygiene.

This is where characters at the extremes of the cleaning spectrum emerge. For every roommate who is cleaning averse, there is an almost uncanny tendency for there to be another who spends hours navel gazing in the bath, while a line of grumpy cohabitants gather outside the locked bathroom waiting for this cleaning obsessive to finish preening.

I would like to believe there is some pay-off, however, for those who tend to find themselves on the outside of the locked bathroom door, as the character who takes up semi-residence in the bathroom is perhaps more likely to spend hours bleaching toilets and cleaning dishes. Sharing a space is all about compromise, so maybe those wasted minutes spent waiting each morning are balanced by the time saved not doing the washing up that the cleaning obsessive gleefully takes care of. You may resent their bossiness and the smugness with which they tell you how much they clean the apartment, but you can reply about being made to wait each day and, hey, you've avoided having to don the rubber gloves.

Of course, if this ideal symmetry does not exist in your household, and the bathroom-hogger is only interested in cleaning themselves and not the communal areas, then it's time to start shamelessly banging on the bathroom door and drawing up time slots and chore sheets. It's amazing how often roommates are forced to resort to these military-like forms to prevent otherwise sensible, mature people from causing grievous bodily harm.

So bathroom hygiene is no laughing matter. It was recently reported that a man in Texas was stabbed at a bar for apparently not washing his hands. Just another example that germs are fatal and worth writing a note or two about.

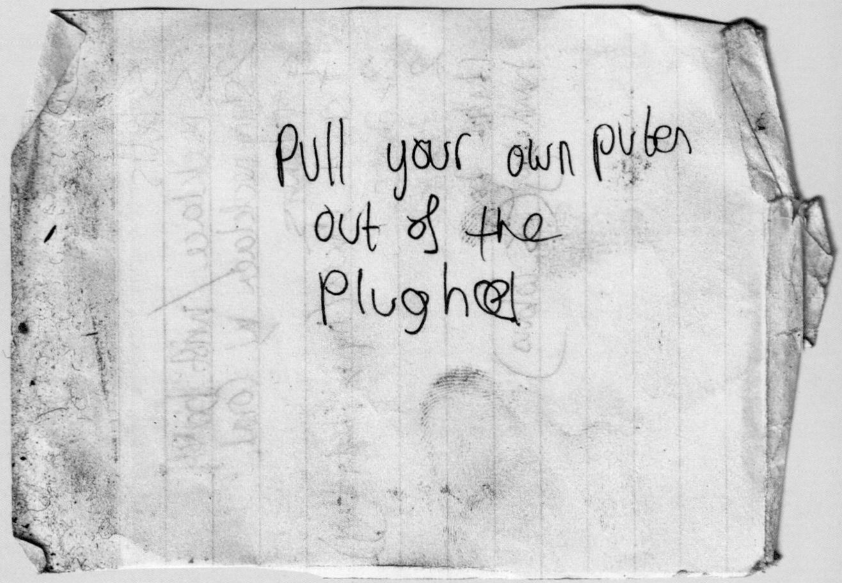
Pull your own pubes
out of the
plughol

The writer was a guy who reported that the woman with whom he shared an apartment had particularly thick, curly hair . . . She was a nice girl in every other aspect apart from her unfortunate bathroom habit. In fact, she was, apparently, a bit of a head-turner. However her dirty secret was that, after taking a bath, she never checked to see if the drain was clear. To quote the writer directly: "What came out of the plug hole was like rope and it was making me feel sick." This note is clearly a cry for help.

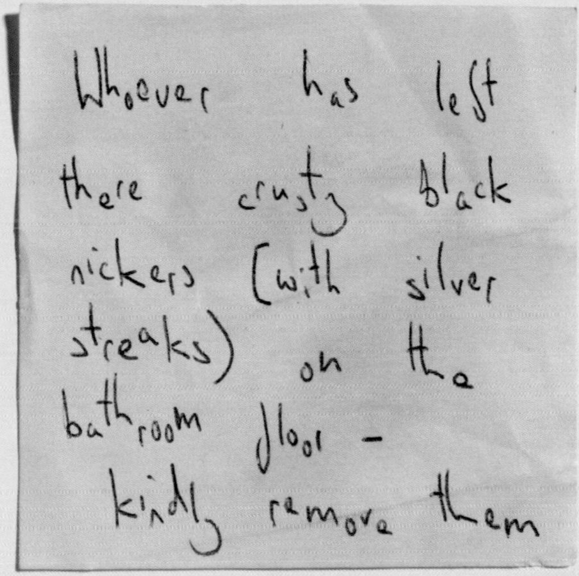
Whoever has left
there crusty black
nickers (with silver
streaks) on the
bathroom floor -
kindly remove them

We all know what is being talked about (or written about) here, but we wish we didn't. While we all have biological functions, we generally don't want to think about them. When I spoke to the man who sent this, he expressed surprise that the girl whose knickers were being discussed cried when she got the note. There is only one word worse than the c-word: it is the other c-word—crusty.

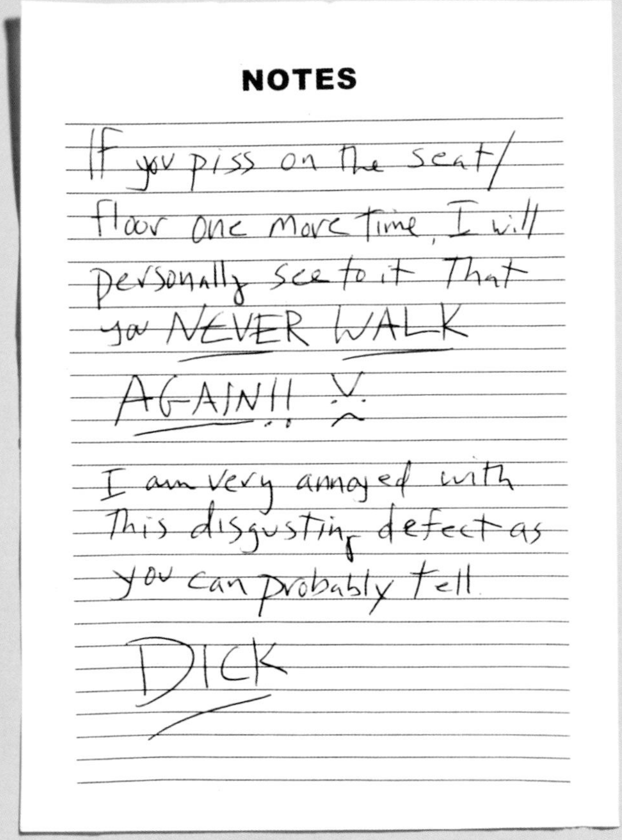
NOTES

If you piss on the seat/
floor one more time, I will
personally see to it That
you NEVER WALK
AGAIN!!

I am very annoyed with
This disgusting defect as
you can probably tell.

DICK

It is beyond me that men are actually equipped with a urinary tract centered in a biological device made for aiming and they still miss. There seems to be a small window of opportunity in a man's life when he can actually aim properly. And just when he is getting into the swing of it, he gets old and blind and clumsy and starts missing again.

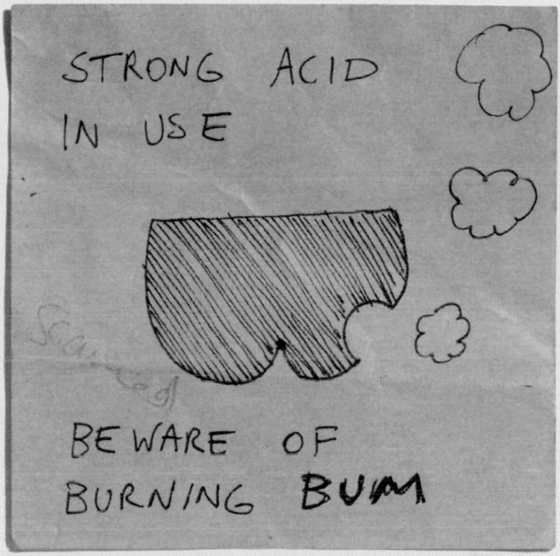
STRONG ACID
IN USE
BEWARE OF
BURNING BUM

This note is considerate on many levels. Not only have they decided to clean the toilet with something so strong it could probably peel paint, they have written *and* illustrated a warning. This has got to be a dream roommate, though one can only wonder why industrial-strength cleaning materials were necessary in the first place.

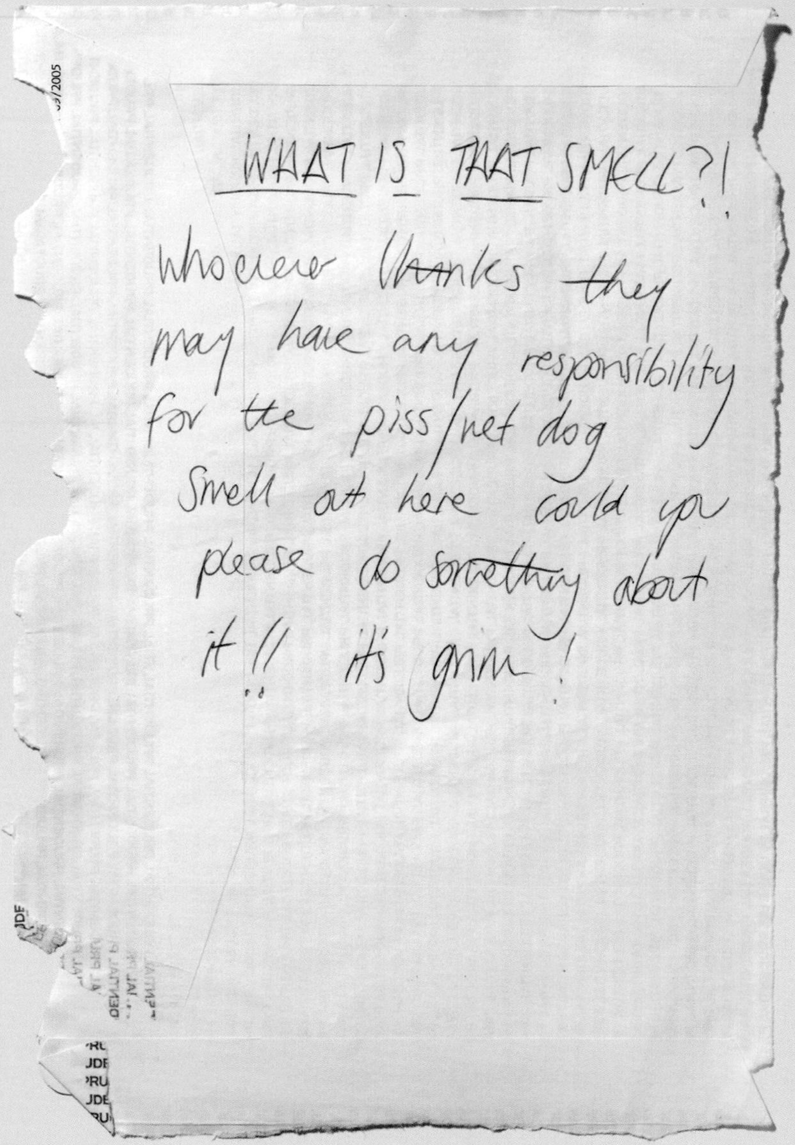

WHAT IS THAT SMELL?!

Whoever thinks they may have any responsibility for the piss/wet dog smell out here could you please do something about it!! it's grim!

Communal areas are often the focus of heated debates. Who buys the light bulbs? Who vacuums the hallway? Who takes responsibility for the garbage? Who deals with the piss/wet dog smell?

You're patient, you try, you leave notes, drop subtle hints, but many are oblivious to tasks that have to be done around the house to make it functional and habitable for all concerned. A major issue is putting out trash for collection. It is amazing how difficult otherwise smart people find this. The scribe of this note has obviously worked tirelessly to get her fellow cohabiters to take part in this task and relieve herself of one of the household chores. So close and yet so far—the bag went out, but just the wrong one.

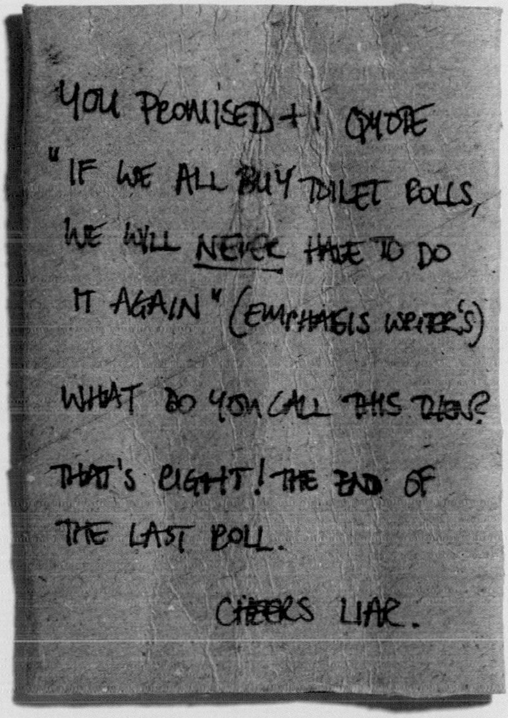
YOU PROMISED + I QUOTE
"IF WE ALL BUY TOILET ROLLS,
WE WILL NEVER HAVE TO DO
IT AGAIN" (EMPHASIS WRITER'S)
WHAT DO YOU CALL THIS THEN?
THAT'S RIGHT! THE END OF
THE LAST ROLL.
CHEERS LIAR.

A favorite old chestnut of communal living and communal lies. Namely that if roommates all buy essentials whenever they go to the shops, the apartment will not run out of stuff. Unfortunately, it is only the conscientious who do it and the non-conscientious who abuse it.

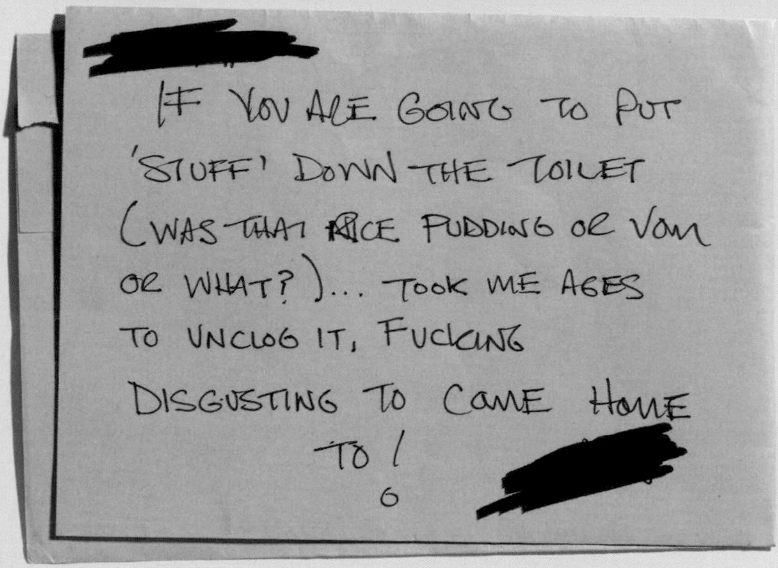
[redacted]
IF YOU ARE GOING TO PUT
'STUFF' DOWN THE TOILET
(WAS THAT RICE PUDDING OR VOM
OR WHAT?)... TOOK ME AGES
TO UNCLOG IT, FUCKING
DISGUSTING TO CAME HOME
TO!
[redacted]
6

Vomit is a difficult subject to bring up. Sorry. Gags aside (sorry again), it can be very awkward. Nearly as bad as throwing-up is someone else finding the evidence. A shameful, hazy night is brought back with full force when someone refers to the bits of a doner kebab they have found floating in the toilet. The rice pudding mentioned in this note is particularly interesting as there is no mention of the cubed carrot that we all know always appears in vomit regardless of what you have eaten.

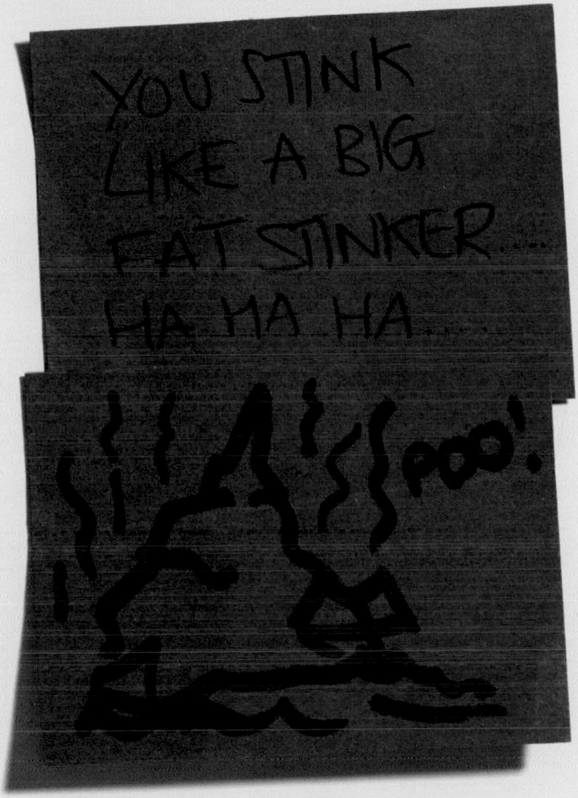
YOU STINK
LIKE A BIG
FAT STINKER....
HA HA HA...
POO!

Humor can often be a good way of broaching a difficult topic. Bodily odors not only fill a room, but can also cling to everyone in that room. Before you know it, you all stink. But how do you address a grown adult who appears not to have worked out how to clean himself? As an alternative to leaving deodorant out, a note like this is clear and to the point. Bravo!

you ok? heard you on
the big white telephone
all night, and a lot of
banging and crashing.
Going out for a full English,
but I am guessing you
wont be up for it.

See you later

"The big white telephone"—I have not heard this euphemism for a long time. The phrase I am accustomed to is a little more elaborate: "on the big white telephone talking to Hughie and Ralph." It's slightly dated now, with more modern favorites such as "a pavement pizza" taking over. I like this note as there is an undertone of Schadenfreude. The author must know the last thing the recipient would want at this stage is a full English breakfast of sausage links, eggs, and fried tomatos. In fact, even the thought will probably have them rushing right back to the toilet. Feigning concern, this note was a successful way of getting someone back for interrupting a good night's sleep.

PLEASE DO NOT DO
BIG SHITS IN
THE TOILET
Thank You

This is one of the rare notes that was sent with an explanation, and one that's not as confusing as it initially sounds. Being a raven-haired beauty, the young lady of the house had a lot of strapping young men visiting her abode. These big, strong guys obviously ate a huge amount to maintain their bulk. Unfortunately the creaking plumbing system had been installed in Victorian times, an era when everyone was shorter and narrower, and probably lived on a lump of coal and two peas a day, meaning their waste was minimal. As a result of several cloggings, it became apparent that, when visiting this lady, it was better to make sure you had done your "big business" beforehand, unless you wanted to spend the rest of the time there with rubber gloves on and a plunger in hand.

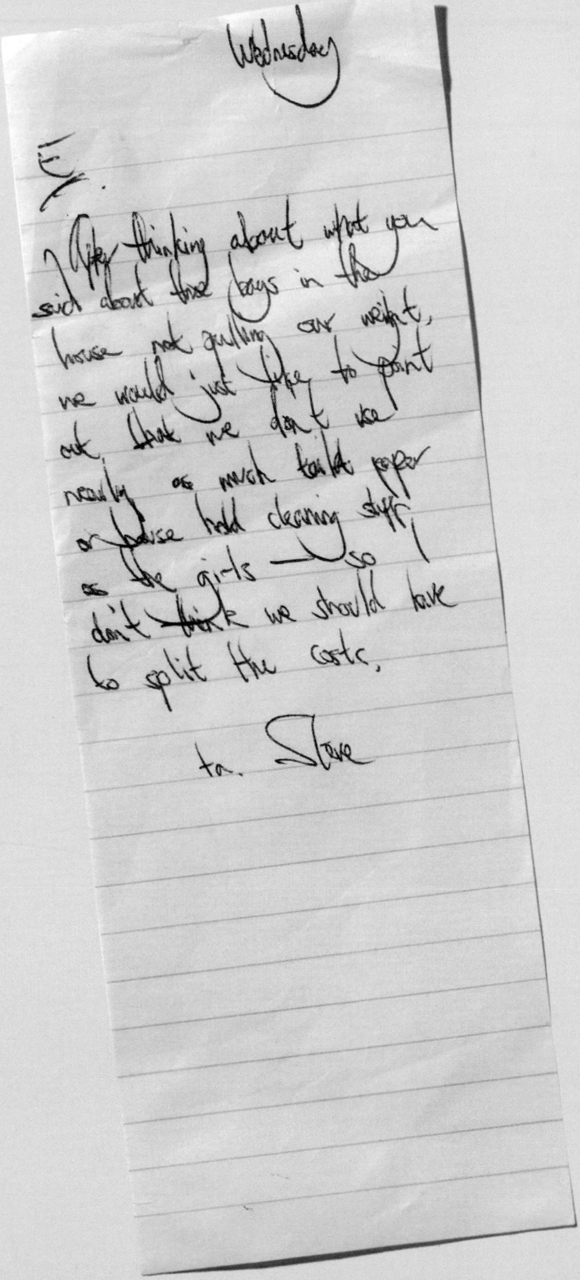

Wednesday

Hi,

Been thinking about what you
said about those boys in the
house not pulling our weight,
we would just like to point
out that we don't use
nearly as much toilet paper
or house hold cleaning stuff
as the girls — so I
don't ~~think~~ we should have
to split the costs.

ta. Steve

Have you been counting? You will now. That's right, counting the sheets—how many sheets of toilet paper you use on every visit. Are you a folder or a crumpler? In doing this book, I have found out the most interesting and personal details about people: the lengths individuals will go to with toilet paper, peeling apart the double ply, wrapping it around a finger (oh God, no). Steve's argument may not be so outlandish as it might appear on first sight. When researching this topic, it has only been men who have confessed to resorting to using, among other things, newspaper and other paperwork. Mind you, maybe women are just not as prepared to admit to it and, who knows, it could be a very efficient way of recycling glossy magazines. Even better, it could be a sweet revenge on the face of some of our beloved celebrities in the gossip rags.

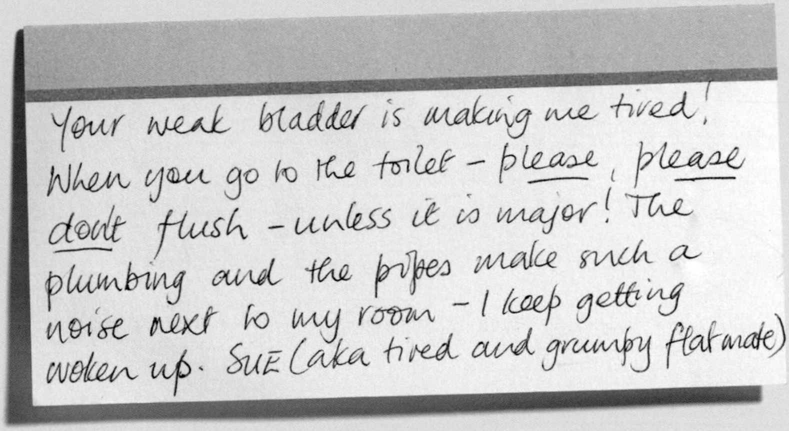
Your weak bladder is making me tired!
When you go to the toilet - please, please
don't flush - unless it is major! The
plumbing and the pipes make such a
noise next to my room - I keep getting
woken up. SUE (aka tired and grumpy flatmate)

What is it about booze that you can just keep going? Ah, that's right, it's addictive. But the most interesting boozing phenomenon is that no matter how much you drink, you always seem to expel double the amount. This can be a tiring pursuit of getting up and blindly stumbling along hallways fumbling with door handles in a desperate search for the bathroom. I have heard many, sadly not apocryphal, stories of gents found peeing in drawers, ashtrays and closets. But as Steve pointed out in a previous note, at least that means they use less toilet paper. Every cloud . . .

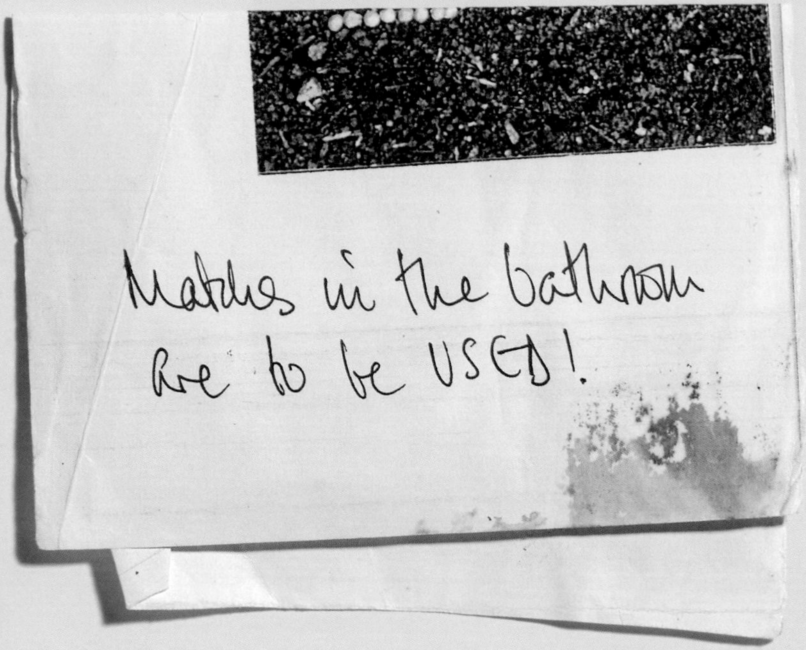
Matches in the bathroom
Are to be USED!

The original air freshener. Never mind your fancy potpourris, candles, or scented solvents; the good old-fashioned match is the best way of burning off any methane that is lingering in the air. Just be sure to keep it away from "the biological methane valve" to avoid seriously unpleasant burns.

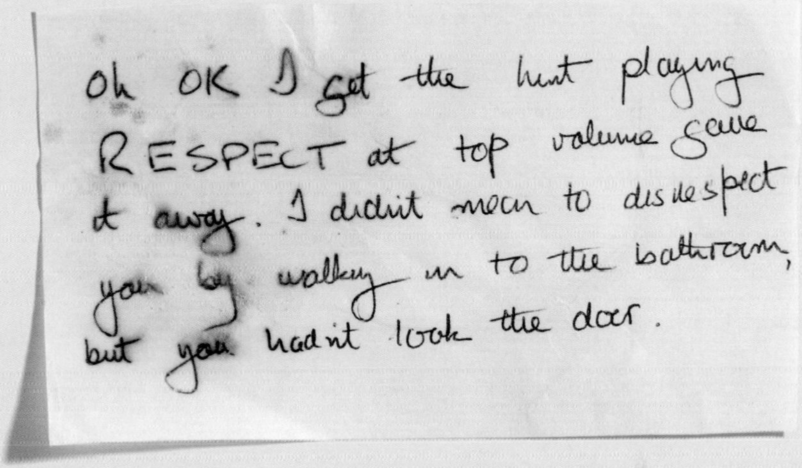
Oh OK I get the hint playing
RESPECT at top volume gave
it away. I didnt mean to disrespect
you by walking in to the bathroom,
but you hadnt lock the door.

I have been inspired. Less confrontational (or more cowardly) than note writing is simply to play music to get your point across. Other possible tracks could be "Welcome to the Monkey House" by the Dandy Warhols, or "[I Hate] Everything About You" by Ugly Kid Joe. Gosh, I feel a compilation CD coming.

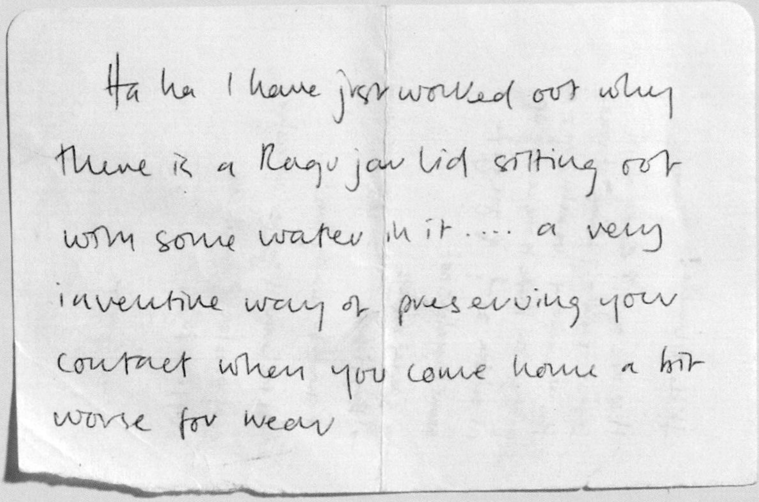

Ha ha I have just worked out why
there is a Ragu jar lid sitting out
with some water in it .... a very
inventive way of preserving your
contact when you come home a bit
worse for wear

Contacts have a whole array of issues associated with them: grit, drying out, and slipping behind your eye into your brain. And after a long day and an even longer night out, it is understandable that having to fiddle around with fluids and small containers, which is not that easy when sober, is not as appealing as simply collapsing into bed. Yet is it worth that extra hour of sleep if it means having your lenses welded to your eyes in the morning? This note offers the perfect solution. It is very straightforward: grab the nearest container, in this case a spaghetti-sauce jar lid, fill lid with some bog-standard water, and decant lenses into the water. Result: useless contact lenses no doubt coated with several billion bacteria. Still, better out than in.

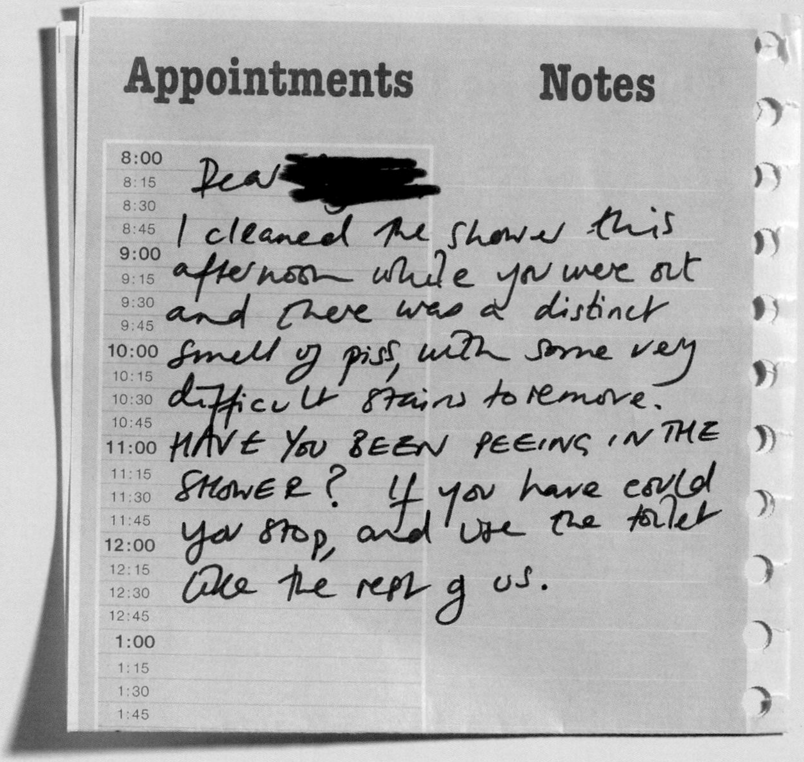
Appointments
Notes
8:00
8:15
8:30
8:45
9:00
9:15
9:30
9:45
10:00
10:15
10:30
10:45
11:00
11:15
11:30
11:45
12:00
12:15
12:30
12:45
1:00
1:15
1:30
1:45
Dear [redacted]
I cleaned the shower this
afternoon while you were out
and there was a distinct
smell of piss, with some very
difficult stains to remove.
HAVE YOU BEEN PEEING IN THE
SHOWER? If you have could
you stop, and use the toilet
like the rest of us.

I read an article not so long ago that reported that Madonna allegedly said (I repeat, allegedly) on a TV show that peeing in the shower is good for you. Apparently it acts as an antiseptic and the enzymes fight off things such as athlete's foot. I have always been a little uneasy about celebrity-endorsed theories since Doctor Atkins died. Pass the carb-packed sandwich, I'm off to buy some bleach.

ASHTRAY NEXT TO
THE BATH – YOU CAN
TELL WHICH IS WHICH
BY THE SIZE
Signed X
(THE ONE WHO USES THE BATH)

This seems very Hugh Hefner—smoking in the bath. I would have thought the logistics of this are quite tricky. Unless you have your very own Playboy Bunnies to hold your, er, cigar, in the bath, would it not be going out all the time? It's hard enough finding the soap in the bath, never mind a lighter and a pack of cigarettes. Probably better just to quit.

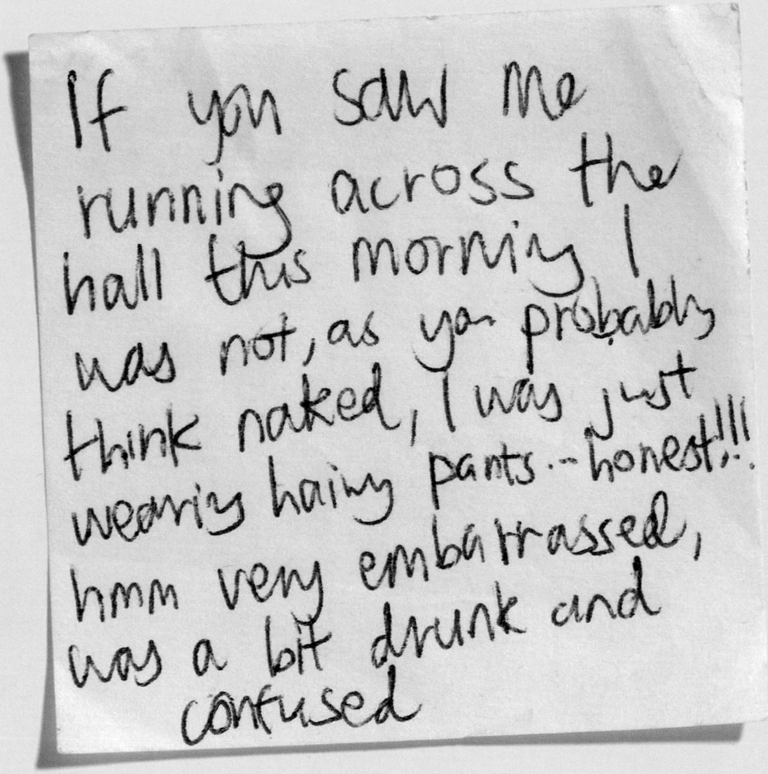
If you saw me
running across the
hall this morning I
was not, as you probably
think naked, I was just
wearing hairy pants...honest!!!
hmm very embarrassed,
was a bit drunk and
confused

My parents grew up in the 1940s and recount horror stories of swimming lessons at local public baths. Besides no heating, caustic soap, and corn plasters in the pool, the worst thing they told me about was swimsuits you could rent. If the thought of sharing these garments is not grim enough, just consider for a moment what they were made of. I am told that before the days of figure-hugging Spandex and Lycra, bathing suits were more of the itchy woollen kind. I can't help thinking of these bathing suits when I read this note. From now on I am going to swim naked and say I am wearing my brown-mohair bikini bottoms. You have been warned.

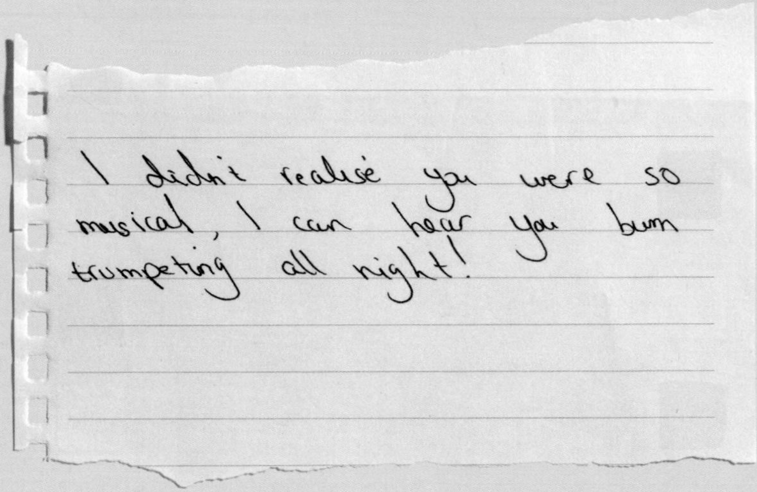
I didn't realise you were so musical, I can hear you bum trumpeting all night!

There is not much you can do about noisy innards. To hear someone else's "bum trumpeting" all night may be irritating, but there is not a lot the player can do, bar stuffing a cork up their—well, you get the idea.

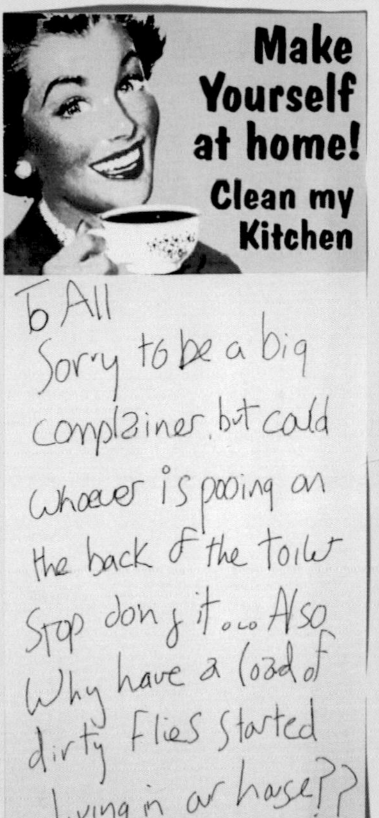
Make Yourself at home!
Clean my Kitchen
To All
Sorry to be a big complainer, but could whoever is pooing on the back of the toilet stop doing it... Also
Why have a load of dirty flies started living in our house??

I don't really think this person is a particularly big complainer. The toilet is for defecating in, so why do the job only ninety percent well and leave a little reminder of what you have been doing in there, in case we didn't know? Some things are private, and what you ate for lunch yesterday should remain your own business. Now let that be the end of it.

I really enjoyed the party
but _haven't_ enjoyed been
the one left to tidy up.
ESPECIALLY as I found
a soiled pair of y fronts
behind the cistern. who
the hell was that, thought
I was going to be sick,

you each owe me at least
a pint.

Sometimes a party can be just that bit *too* exciting. It puts a lot of pressure on your body: copious amounts of liquid, probably dodgy food, smoking like a beagle, and the increasingly common drug-induced runs. There is probably nothing worse. You take a mood-enhancing something or other and suddenly it all seems great; you're floating, and you're the life and soul of the party, dancing like you're fluid, being as funny and witty as Oscar Wilde. And then it happens. You feel everything in your stomach move down a notch or two and the curry you had a couple of hours ago is now resting like lead and wants out. You look over and, as with all good parties, there is a huge line outside the toilets, mostly made up of pretty girls in twos. By the time you eventually reach the almost mythical toilet, things go from bad to much, much worse. This note tells the rest of the story.

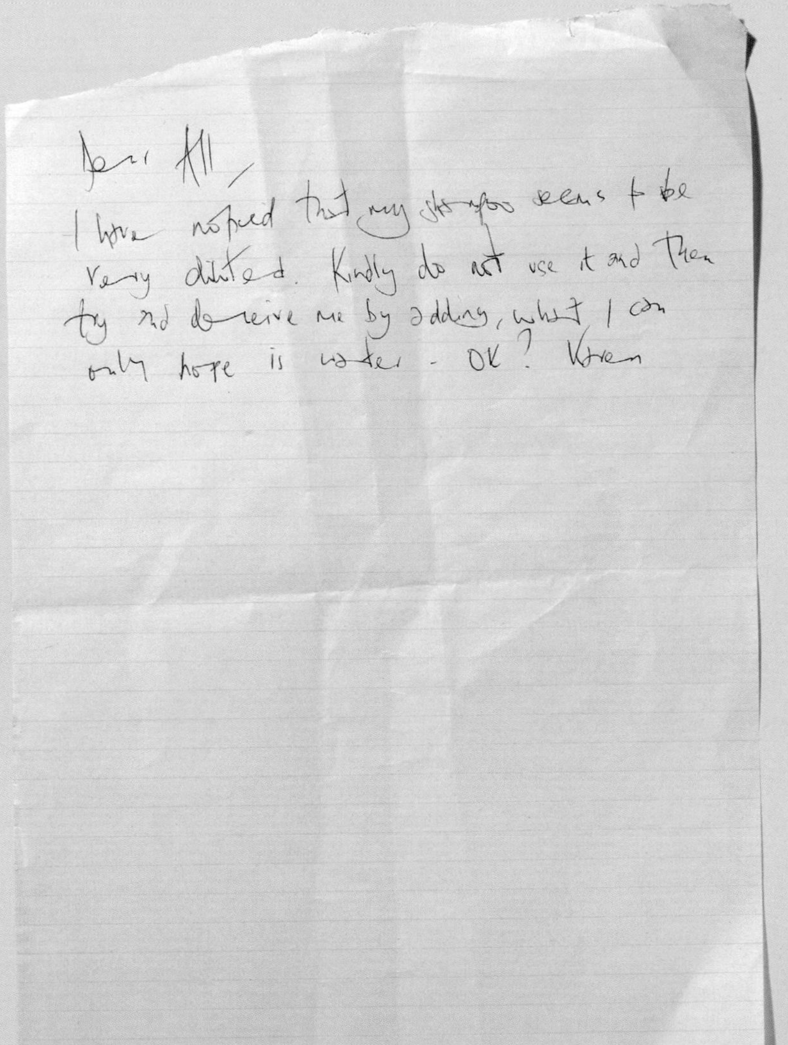
Dear All,
I have noticed that my shampoo seems to be very diluted. Kindly do not use it and then try and deceive me by adding, what I can only hope is water - OK? Karen

I have heard of people topping up miniatures of vodka in minibars at hotels with water, but shampoo? That is truly cheap. The added element of hope in this note panics me, especially after having read a report of a man who was caught peeing in his work colleagues' communal coffee machine. I too can only hope that Karen has been washing her hair with a water and shampoo combination. Liquids such as beer are apparently good for your coiffure, but urine I have yet to see as a crucial new ingredient in one of those complicated shampoo adverts from "laboratories herbal hair defineutraline" or the likes. Bet Karen's hair looks great, but smells like—well, like she didn't just step out of a salon.

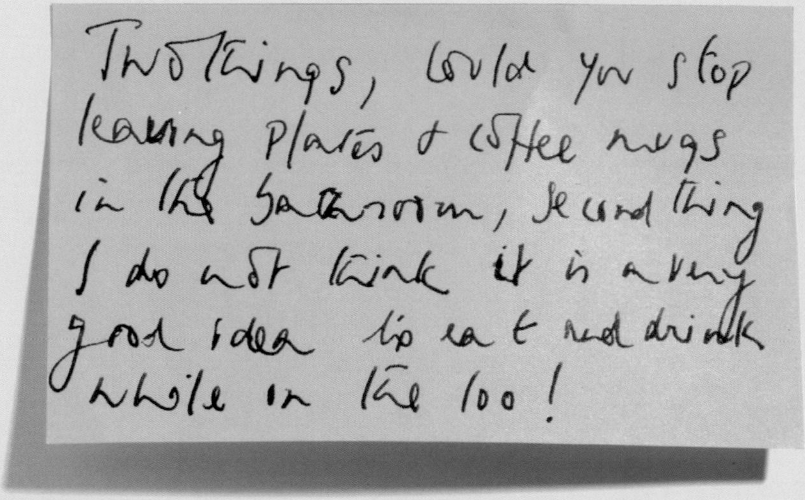
Two things, could you stop
leaving plates & coffee mugs
in the bathroom, second thing
I do not think it is a very
good idea to eat and drink
while in the loo!

I wonder if anyone has rented out their bathroom? It has all the necessary amenities, such as running water and a place to sleep, although not really anything for cooking, unless you are happy to turn on the shower and steam your food.

IMPORTANT!
Is my toothbrush
in your room?
Please leave by
my door
If not, AARGH!
xxxx

How the hell does a toothbrush end up in someone else's room? It can't really be an accident. So let's see, you picked up the wrong toothbrush (and didn't notice? They are color coded, dammit!) and, while cleaning your teeth, you sauntered out of the bathroom into the bedroom where you finished brushing (and didn't rinse or anything?) and, oh, you got distracted and just left it there? The only other explanation is these two are secretly having a relationship, and their preference is to brush each other's teeth mid-foreplay. (Oooh, I love it when you flouridate my molars.) Yes, that is the only answer.

"I lick my cheese."

FOOD AND OTHER NOTES FROM THE KITCHEN

We all think we have the best taste, but one man's meal is another's leftovers. And the way and what we eat is very personal and can structure a day, so people can be very protective about their food. It's a primal instinct. Needless to say, vegetarians, vegans, those who are lactose intolerant, and old-school junk-eaters do not survive well in the same house.

Many of these note writers are on a diet. If you are on a diet, everyone is affected. If you have ever included mung beans into your five portions of fruit and veggies a day, you will be aware of the amazing chemical reactions they induce in the stomach. Gaseous, grumpy, and minus two hundred calories, the "dieter" comes home to find the kitchen in disarray. It takes a strong character to resist leaving a note, or even eating the notepad. The lady on the TV who examines your poo and the man who makes juices both have a lot to answer for. I would like to know how many households have been woken by the dulcet tones of a smoothie machine pulsing away at 6:30 A.M. before a detoxifying run. Mind you, it's not just the dieters that are smelly. Have you ever opened a pack of wafer-thin turkey? It smells like farts. Why? But frankly, who cares—it serves you right for purchasing something described as "80% meat" (what the hell is the other 20%?).

Then there is the "foodie"—someone who knows their chard from their kale. Pretensions aside, foodies are actually just greedy. They like gorging. Mind you, it isn't the foodies who are suffering from the recent obesity problems. The foodies are at least eating products that have some vague resemblance to food. The food they eat hasn't been shaped into a rectangle or hilarious twizzle shape. No the people who are getting fat beyond the supermarkets' wildest dreams are the microwave-dinner diners. These types do not spend long periods of time in the kitchen, as there is no preparation involved with their food—apart from unwelding plastic food from a plastic container. Everything has already been done for them and, in their homes, the busiest door is that of the freezer. In fact, you could be forgiven for mistaking their behind for their face, as the only thing you ever see of them is their ass hanging out of the freezer while they forage for more frozen foods.

Whether it is a case of too much or too little, food can be an obsession and so it is a fertile ground for note writing. If you are addicted to anything, having it or depriving yourself of it can send you over the edge.

STOP BURNING THINGS

It's just rude, isn't it, to keep setting the apartment on fire. It's really quite discourteous.

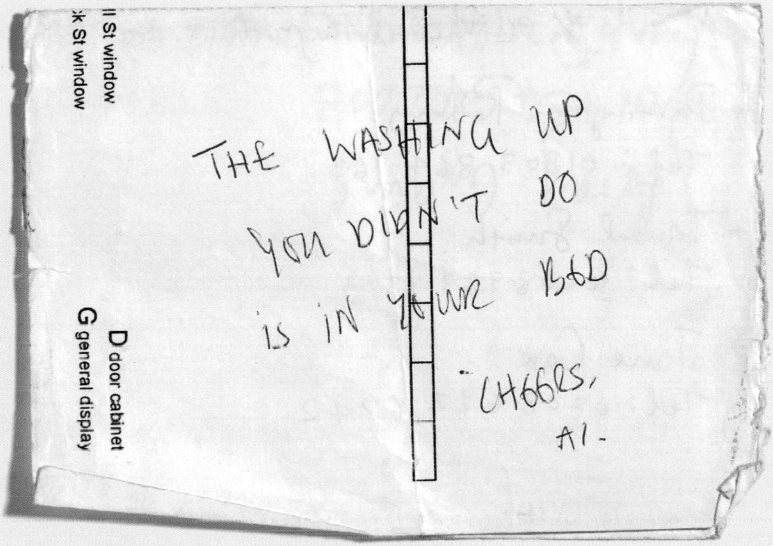
ll St window
k St window
THE WASHING UP
YOU DIDN'T DO
IS IN YOUR BED
CHEERS,
AL.
D door cabinet
G general display

While researching this book, I found out that there are a range of tips that have become almost folklore for tackling difficult cohabiting issues. Putting washing-up in the bed of a non-washer-upper is one of them. From where these tips originate I do not know—they must be passed from generation to generation, or maybe there are groups of very clean people meeting to discuss tried and tested techniques. My tip is: use paper plates. Failing that, resort to the technique employed by one particularly skanky individual who lived with a friend—he covered dirty plates with tinfoil before using them again to deposit his nightly take-out onto them.

Please don't soak my
stuff that's made out
of wood – it bends +
cracks them when
the fibres get full
of water
cheers!

Cheers indeed. But this was both written and received with a sense of desperation. This person was so pedantic that every day there was a new message. It got to the point where the roommates dreaded coming home or waking up, as there would be another little scrap of paper waiting for them. The worst thing was that you often didn't even know what you had done . . .

Whoever eats my cheese.... I LICK IT!!
Ha Ha.
So do I!

Touché. Strangely I have heard of this kind of behavior before. Very primitive—like marking your territory. It works. I wouldn't go near this fridge even if my life depended on it.

PLEASE DONT TURN THIS INTO AN ARGUMENT
AS IT NEEDNT BE
IF WE CAN BE MATURE ABOUT THIS

IT WOULD BE RIDICULOUS FOR EACH
OF US TO HAVE TO LABEL ALL OUR
BELONGINGS IN THE FLAT

ALL I AM ASKING IS THAT WHEN YOUR
BOYFRIEND FINDS SOMETHING HE WANTS
TO THROW AWAY BUT DOESNT BELONG
TO HIM

HE ASKS THE PERSON WHO OWNS IT FIRST

WE CAN AVOID ANY UNPLEASANT FEELING
IN THE FLAT IF WE JUST OBSERVE
COMMON COURTESY, AND WE ALL
WANT TO LIVE IN A FLAT THAT HAS
A GOOD FEELING ABOUT IT

I. AM SURE YOU CAN UNDERSTAND THIS
FROM MY POINT OF VIEW, AND WE CAN
SORT THIS OUT POLITELY

HAVE A GOOD EASTER

[redacted]

"We can be mature about this," or "I don't want this to be a big problem" etc, is generally to be reread as "this is going to be a huge problem." To be compelled to commit it to paper rather than muttering it under your breath on your own means you can't be mature about it. It *is* going to be an argument and you are *not* sorry about it.

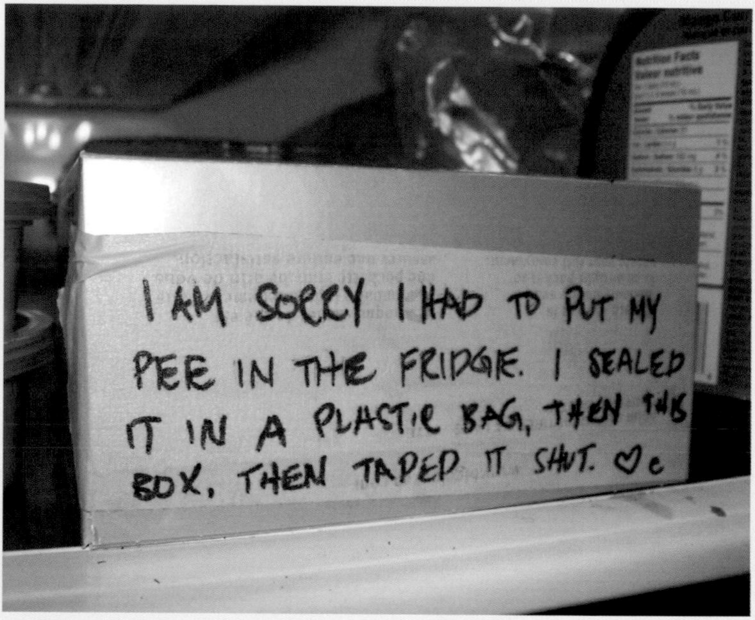
I AM SORRY I HAD TO PUT MY PEE IN THE FRIDGE. I SEALED IT IN A PLASTIC BAG, THEN THIS BOX, THEN TAPED IT SHUT. ♡c

Oh for the love of God, you just don't . . . you just wouldn't. I mean, would you? At least they had the decency to put it into a container that couldn't be mixed up for an apple juice or a particularly tangy vinaigrette.

If undelivered please return to P.O. Box 60 Halifax West Yorkshire HX1 2RG
Has anyone seen the kitchen??

This is a work of genius. Funny, short, and to the point, it sums up what appears to be a scenario full of despair. I think a very apt reply to this note would be: can you remember where you last saw it? Anyway, it sounds as though this kitchen isn't so much used as abused. It conjures up images of neon-orange sweet-and-sour-sauce-stained worktops, weeks of ungluing noodles from plates, and using a knife to clean the floor.

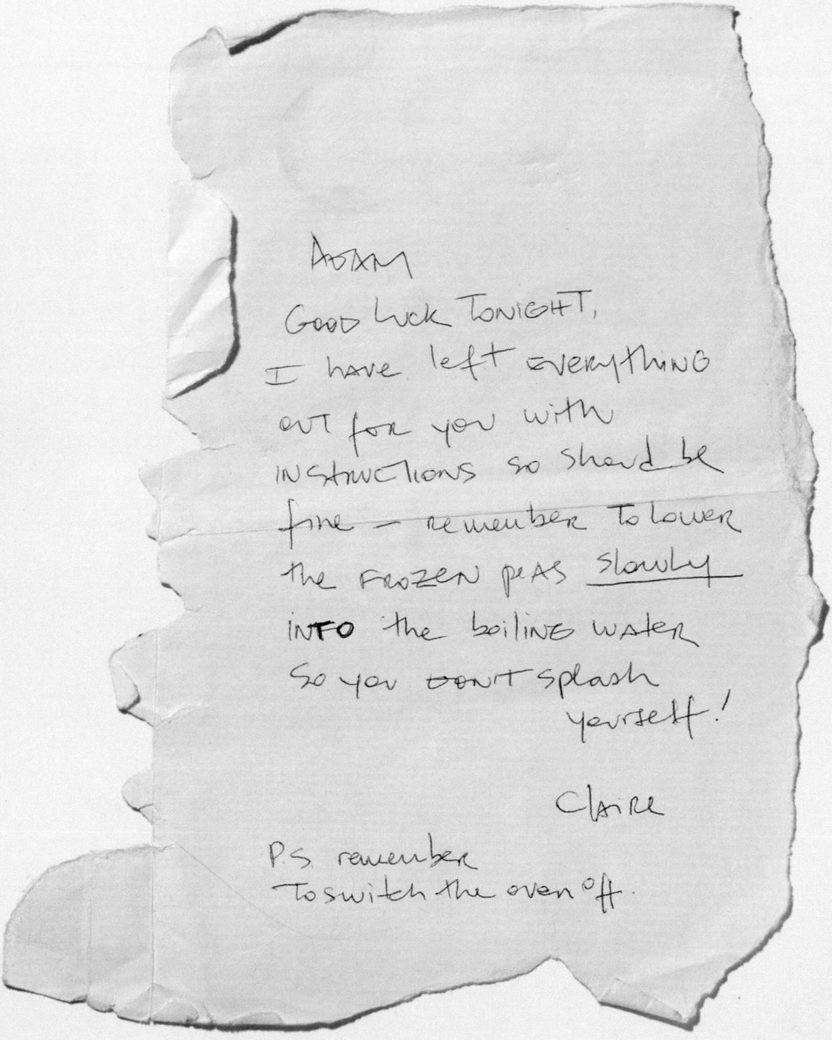

ADAM

GOOD LUCK TONIGHT,
I have left everything
OUT for you with
INSTRUCTIONS so should be
fine – remember To lower
the FROZEN PEAS slowly
INFO the boiling water
so you DON'T splash
yourself!

Claire

P.S. remember
To switch the oven off.

There is a fine line between being helpful and coming across like a control freak. I think Claire might have crossed that line.

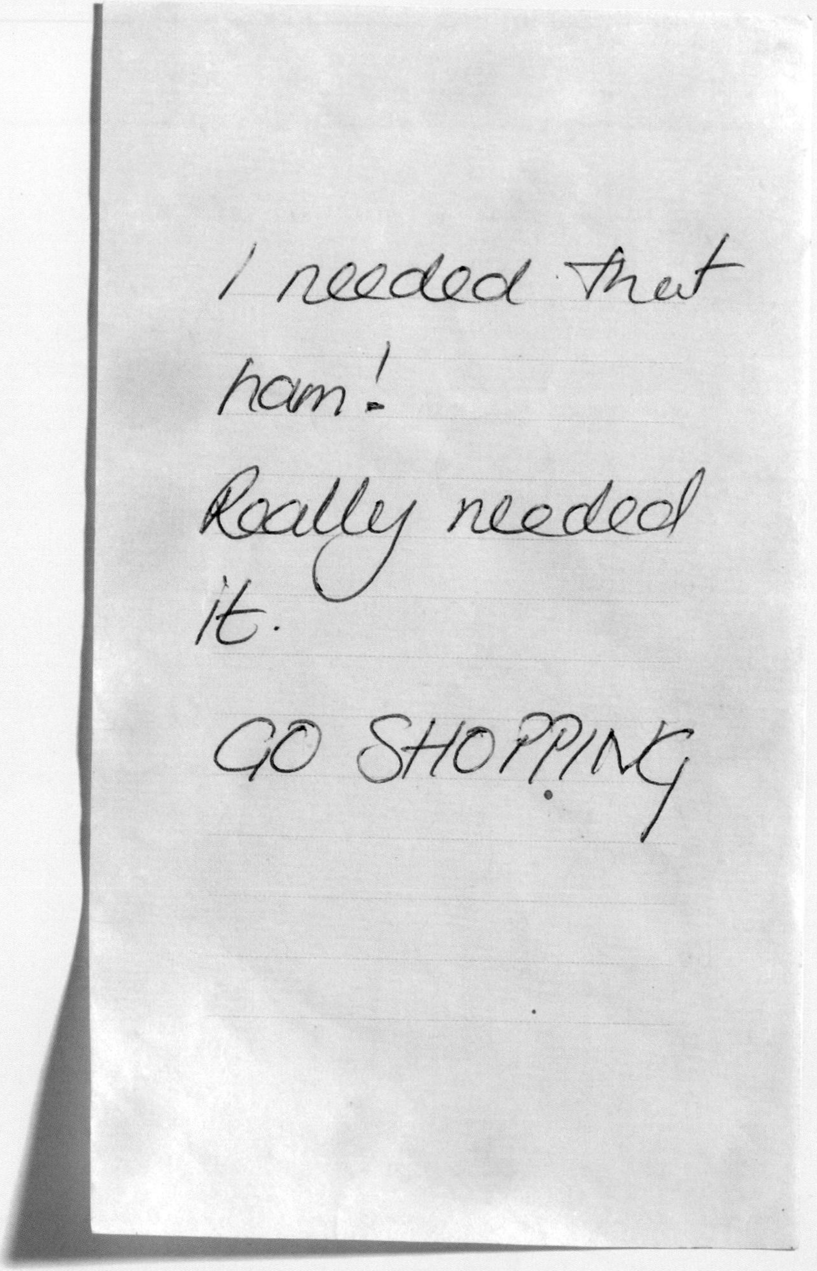
I needed that
ham!
Really needed
it.
GO SHOPPING

There is an explanation to this note. The recipient said the writer was convinced other roommates were stealing her food, which is understandably annoying, especially if you "really need it." (Was she basing a whole meal round a slice of ham?) The reality, however, according to my source, was rather different. Apparently nothing had been taken, especially as the other roommates were both vegetarian. A ham paranoia had set in. Not only had vegetarians stolen her ham, but they had stolen it when she *really* needed it. It had been a Ham Emergency.

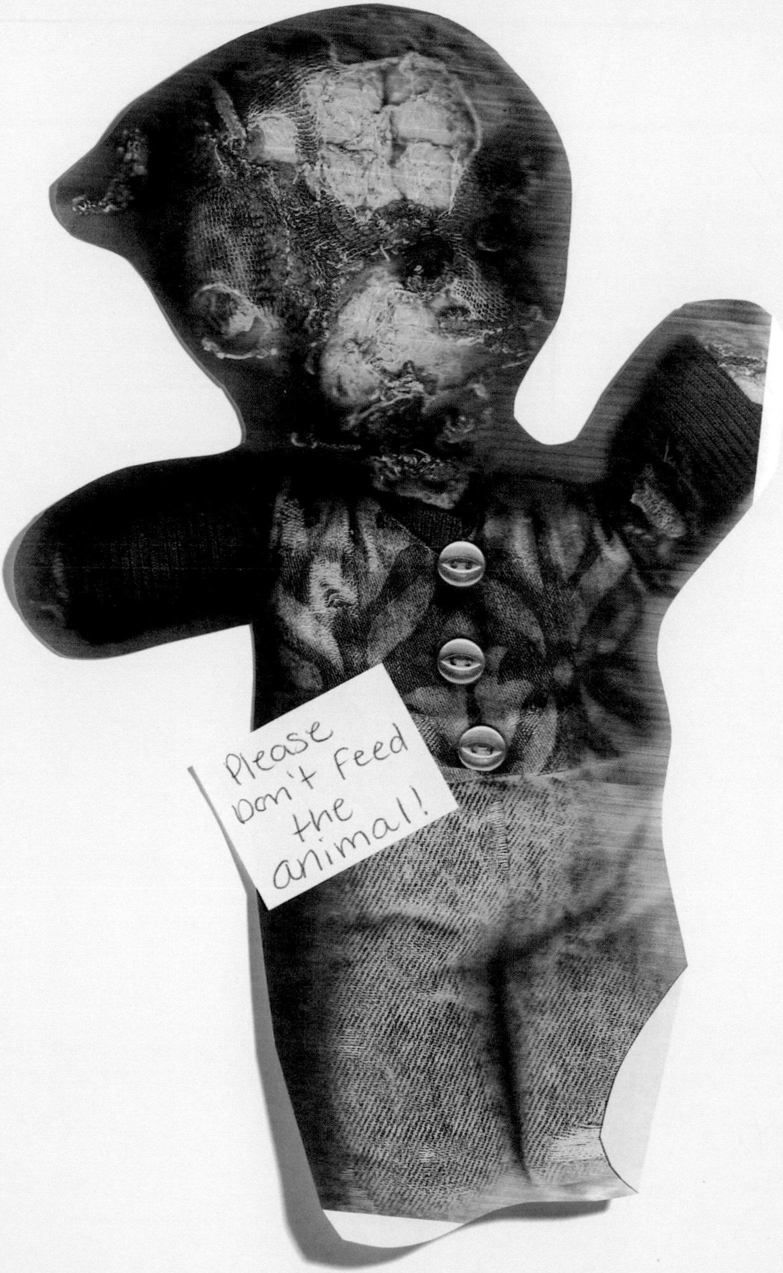
Please
Don't Feed
the
animal!

They say the difference between humans and animals is that humans have a conscience. Living together sometimes suggests otherwise. Roommates may take on a human shape, but their habits, especially eating habits, sometimes suggest they are closer to a feral creature than a human. I have visions of frightened roommates slipping wafer-thin turkey under this person's door rather than risk unleashing him on the rest of the apartment. In fact, he probably hasn't come out of his room all winter, preferring to survive on the small morsels of food caught in his beard.

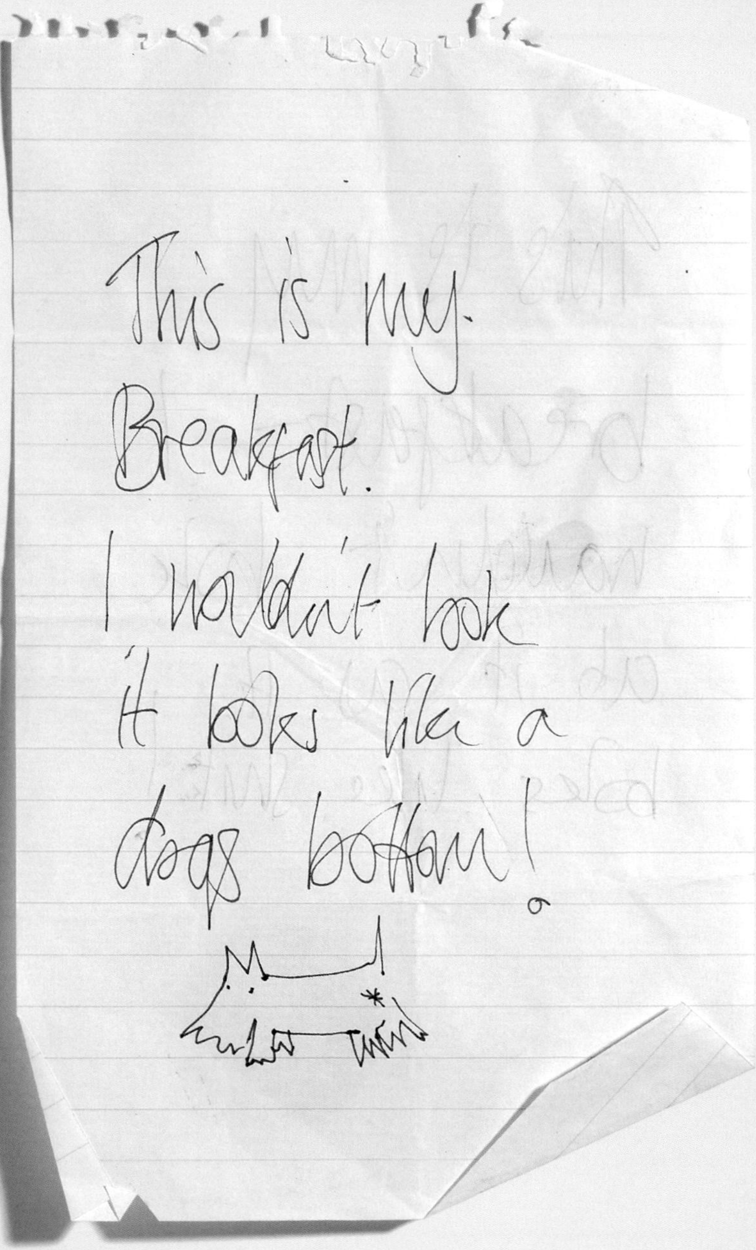

This is my
Breakfast.
I wouldn't look
it looks like a
dogs bottom!

I am informed that the breakfast in question was a bran, muesli, and cranberry-based concoction. Good for the body, but not so pleasant on the eye. The note is worryingly descriptive, but a cunning way to put people off from stealing your cereal.

People WASH your shit!
Thank you
A sink
dirty plates
a happy home.

It might not be particularly eloquent, but you can definitely feel the anger in this note. I am not quite sure what the "shit" refers to, but I can only guess and hope from the illustration that it means washing the dishes, as this tends to be one of the main sources of argument in shared accommodation. There seems to be a little back-pedalling with the venom, as there is a slightly meek "thank you" added at the end, though that could just be sarcasm.

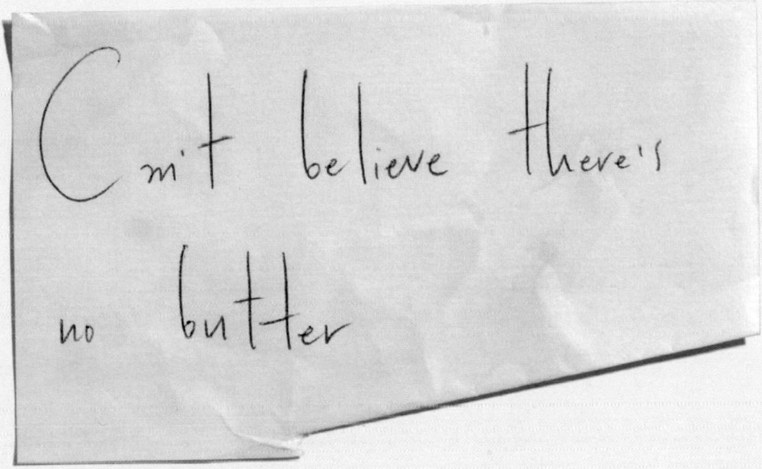
Can't believe there's
no butter

I love this inventive use of an advertising slogan here. OK, so they might not have any fat left to coat their toast, but at least they still have their sense of humor.

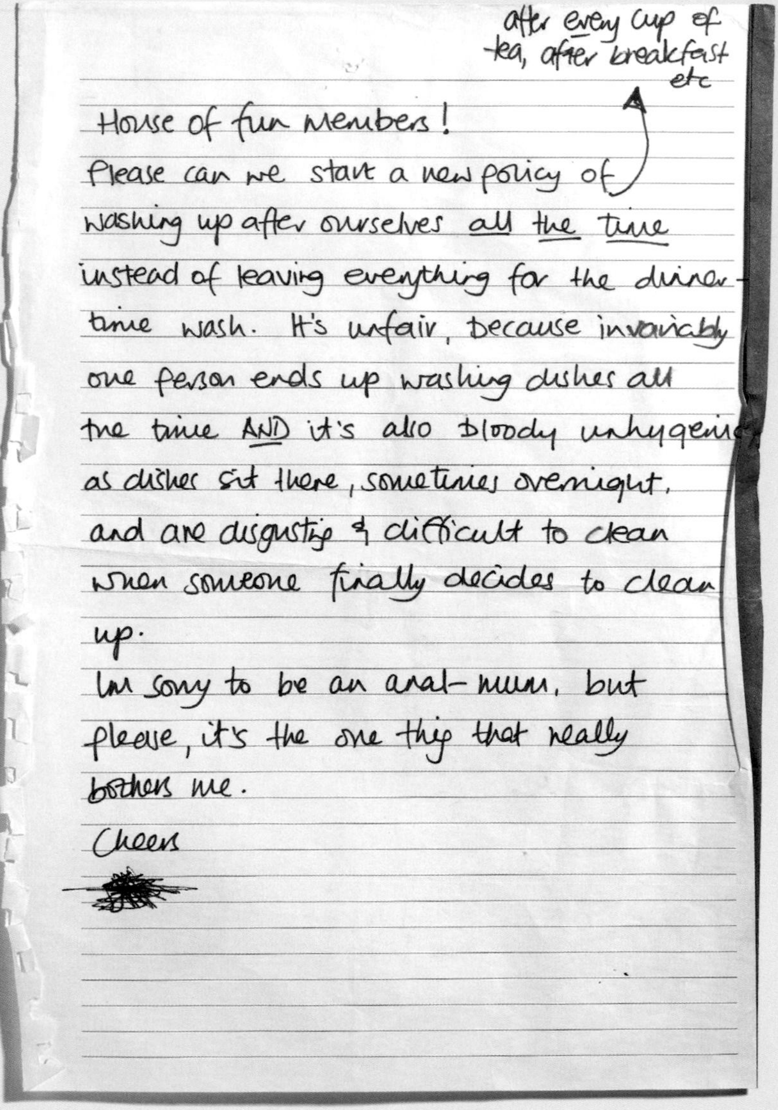

after every cup of tea, after breakfast etc

House of fun members!

Please can we start a new policy of washing up after ourselves all the time instead of leaving everything for the dinner-time wash. It's unfair, because invariably one person ends up washing dishes all the time AND it's also bloody unhygenic as dishes sit there, sometimes overnight, and are disgusting & difficult to clean when someone finally decides to clean up.

I'm sorry to be an anal-mum, but please, it's the one thing that really bothers me.

Cheers

[redacted]

House of Fun? House of Fun? The irony. I don't think there is much fun going on in this house. More often than not, notes such as these contain lots of apologies about bringing the issue to attention. You know, the type that begins with: "I'm embarrassed to mention this, but . . . ," "I can't believe I'm writing this, but . . . ," or "I'm a complete a**hole which is why I'm writing and not talking to you, but . . ." (well, maybe ignore the last one). The point is, these are empty apologies, as the writer clearly still feels compelled to write the note and doesn't seem to have realized that the awkwardness a note can cause is worse than the problem written about in the first place. Also check out the use of the word "policy," which sounds more like the Houses of Parliament than a House of Fun . . .

Hi Guys,

Have been working
on one of my cake
recipies this after
noon, would love to
hear your opinion
on how to make it really
scrummy. Help
yourself, and tell me
what you think...
not enough Ginger?

Making cakes? Scrummy? Enough ginger? I imagine this is the kind of note Nigella Lawson once wrote to her flatmates. It seems to come from another age, when people drank root beer and went on hayrides instead of snorting suspicious powders before an evening of dogging. Scrummy!

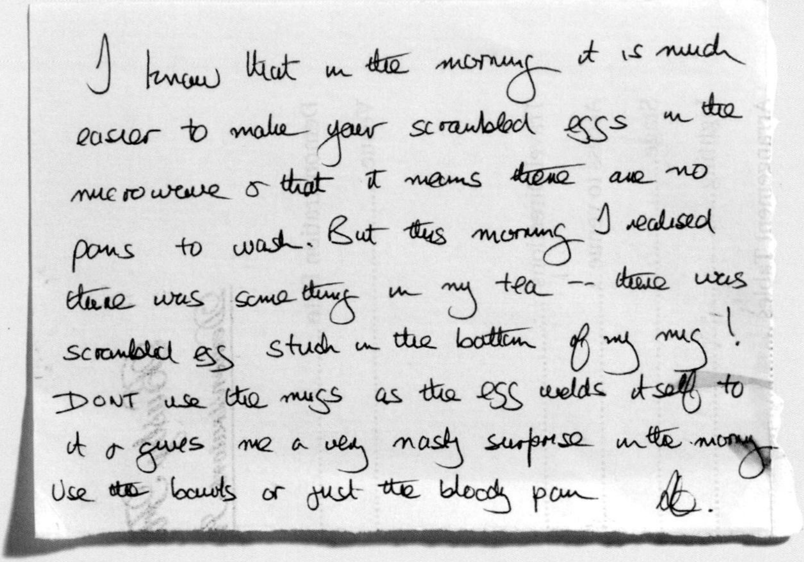
I know that in the morning it is much
easier to make your scrambled eggs in the
microwave & that it means there are no
pans to wash. But this morning I realised
there was something in my tea -- there was
scrambled egg stuck in the bottom of my mug!
DONT use the mugs as the egg welds itself to
it & gives me a very nasty surprise in the morning.
Use the bowls or just the bloody pan

Often when I am reading these notes, I can't help feeling there must be more important issues in the world to care about. Missing ham, licked cheese—they're hardly international crises. But I can understand why the writer lost her sense of humor here. The last thing you need when you stumble down to the kitchen in the morning, half-asleep, is to be confronted with a strange fungus-like object in the bottom of your tea mug. People's stomachs aren't at their strongest at that hour and a new type of lumpy egg-flavored morning beverage is not going to help matters.

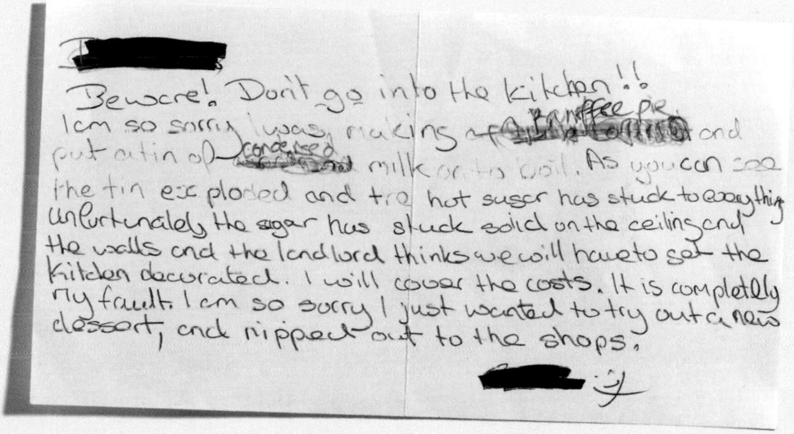
[redacted]
Beware! Don't go into the kitchen!!
I am so sorry I was making Banoffee pie and put a tin of condensed milk on to boil. As you can see the tin exploded and the hot sugar has stuck to everything. Unfortunately the sugar has stuck solid on the ceiling and the walls and the landlord thinks we will have to get the kitchen decorated. I will cover the costs. It is completely my fault. I am so sorry I just wanted to try out a new dessert, and nipped out to the shops.
[redacted] :-)

I have always been a little anxious about dying a comical death. Being consumed by hot, sticky condensed milk is a death that is, yes, wait for it, bittersweet. This note points out how dangerous (and expensive) this situation could be. I just can't help thinking this would be a fitting death for Martha Stewart.

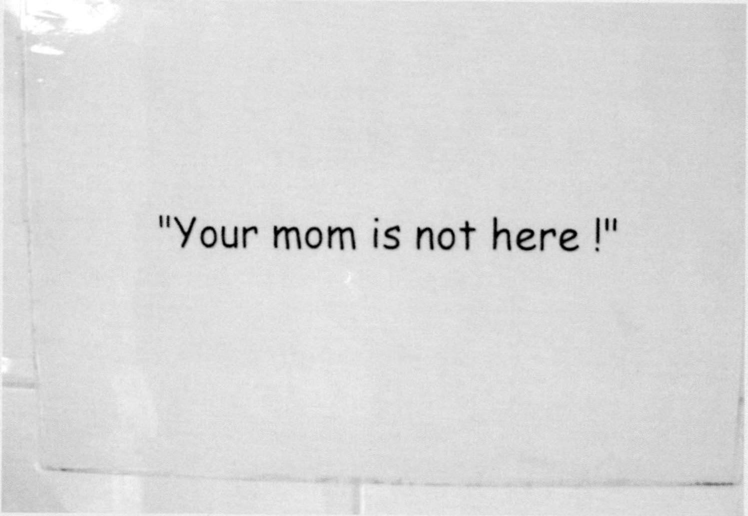
"Your mom is not here !"

Mom may not be here, but someone has gone to a lot of trouble to have this note printed and laminated. This is taking note writing to a new and, to my mind, scarily professional level.

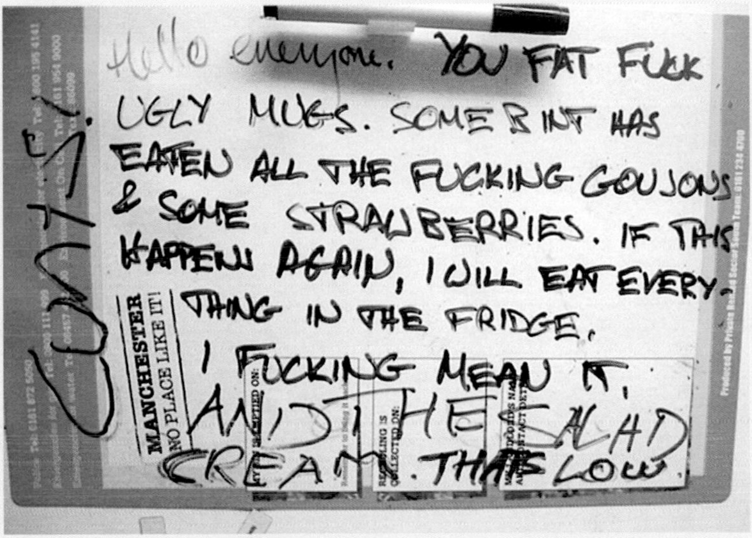
Hello everyone. YOU FAT FUCK UGLY MUGS. SOME BINT HAS EATEN ALL THE FUCKING GOUJONS & SOME STRAWBERRIES. IF THIS HAPPENS AGAIN, I WILL EAT EVERY-THING IN THE FRIDGE.
I FUCKING MEAN IT.
AND THE SALAD CREAM. THAT'S LOW.
CUNTS!
MANCHESTER
NO PLACE LIKE IT!

I can't believe just how pissed off this person is. They seem terribly posh—goujons and strawberries? Is this Donald Trump's fridge? But for all the foul language, the big threat is (oooooh, wait for it; scary scary) they "will eat everything in the fridge." I would pay to see that, especially if this is a fridge that stores pee. (See note on page 122.)

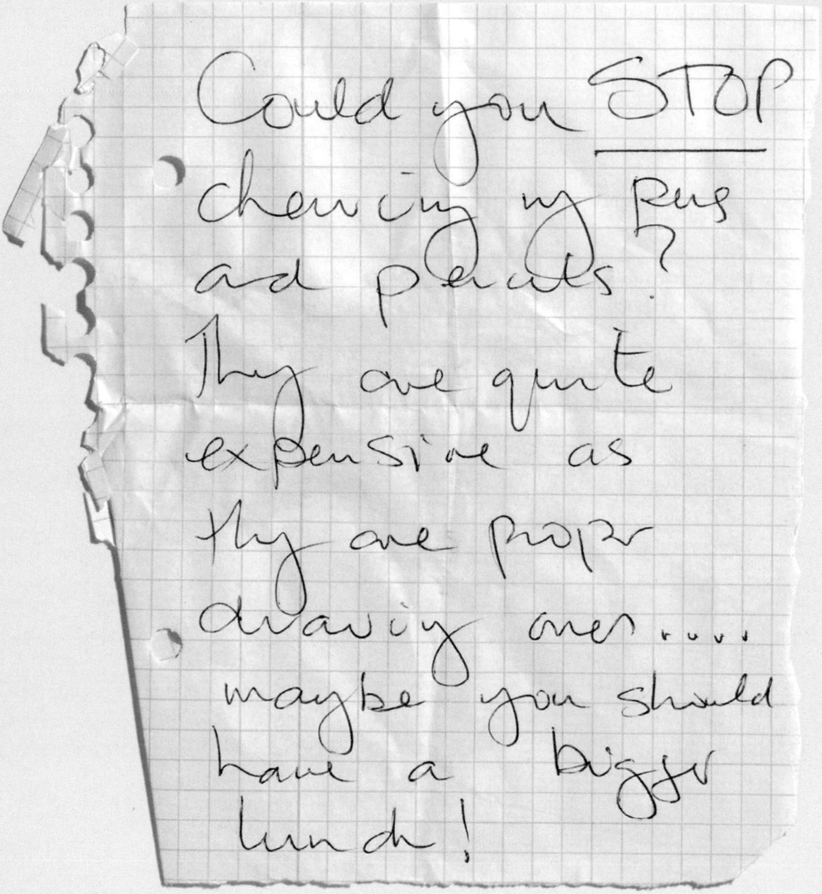
Could you STOP
chewing my pens
and pencils?
They are quite
expensive as
they are proper
drawing ones.....
maybe you should
have a bigger
lunch!

This is a nasty habit. You never know where a pen or pencil has been. I hazard a guess in someone's hand, and that alone is enough to make you stop chewing.

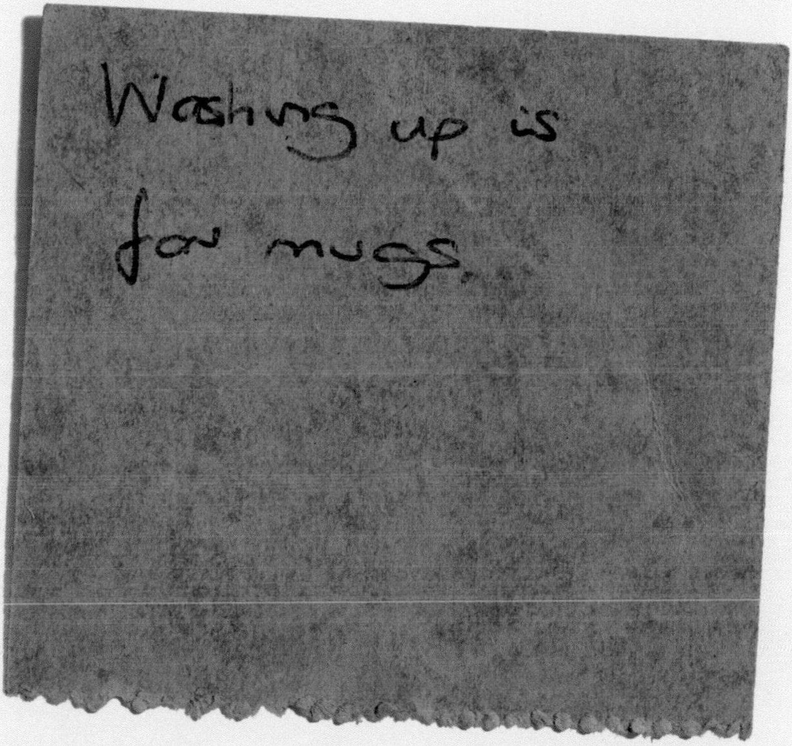
Washing up is
for mugs.

This note stands alone. Too funny to argue with.

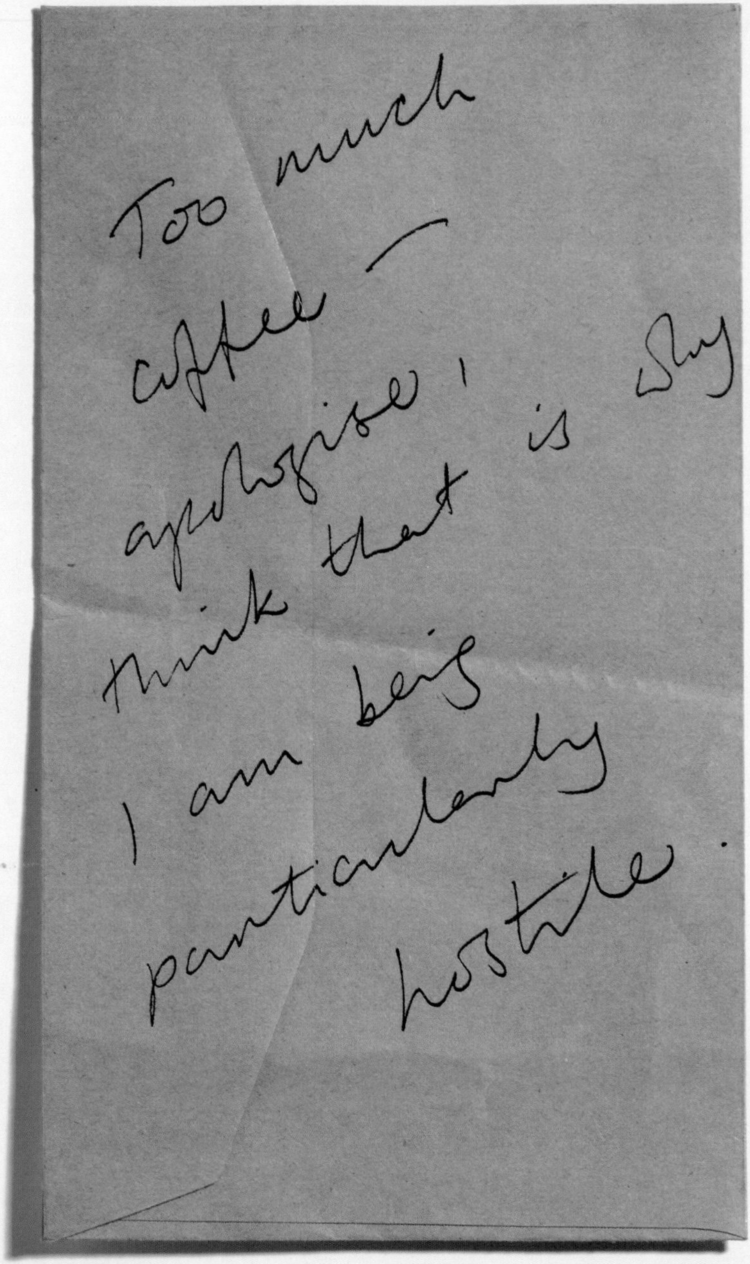
Too much
coffee —
apologise !
think that is why
I am being
particularly
hostile .

One of the most common worldwide addictions is to caffeine. But it's not all just about lattes and skinny mochas. My favorite caffeine product is a pair of stockings available on the Internet that contain caffeine "micro-capsules" that are activated by body heat. (They stimulate cells and burn fat before you ask.) I guess anything is worth a try.

This note is especially interesting, as the writer knows they are hostile but just can't stop drinking coffee—this is a true addict. I wonder if they were wearing the stockings at the time to get a double shot?

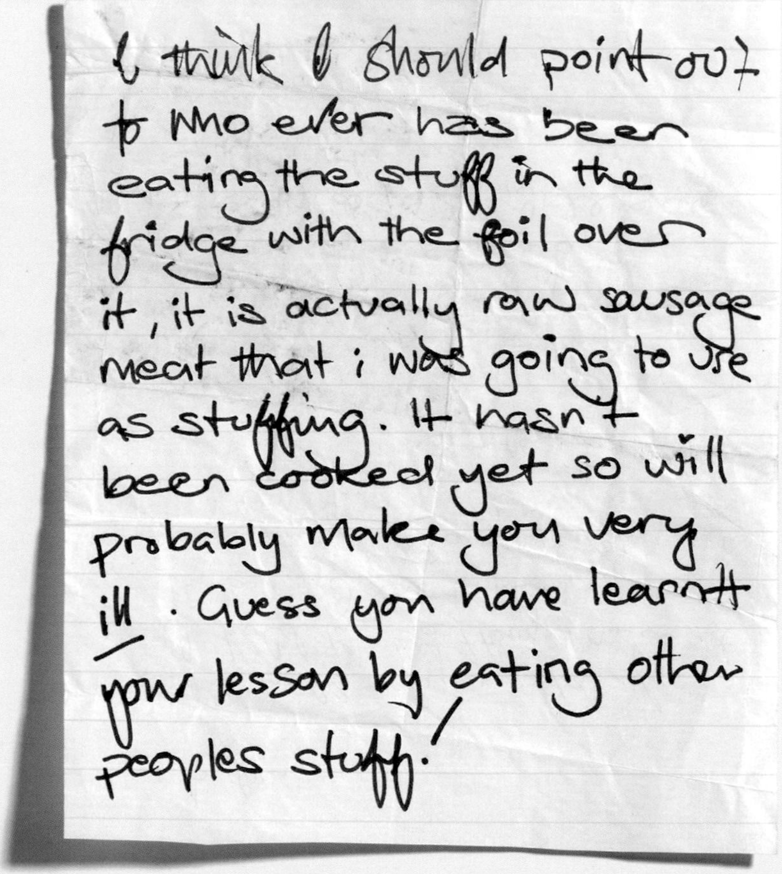

I think I should point out
to who ever has been
eating the stuff in the
fridge with the foil over
it, it is actually raw sausage
meat that i was going to use
as stuffing. It hasn't
been cooked yet so will
probably make you very
ill. Guess you have learnt
your lesson by eating other
peoples stuff!

I like to think of this note's recipient in a dark kitchen, the only light coming from the open fridge that they are squatting in front of, scooping small balls of the soft, moist substance into their mouth with their fingers. Suddenly they notice the note. They stop their gorging, removing their hand from under the foil, careful not to make a noise. Their eyes frantically scan down the note, locking on the word "raw." They feel a horrible sensation. Not only have they been "caught" with their hands in someone else's food, but it has just dawned on them that a ball of raw flesh is swilling around their stomach. Cold sweats, groaning noises from all orifices; this is more than a lesson. This is a brutal, possibly fatal punishment.

Someone
ate my Pasta!
I'm hungry.

This is a sorrowful state of affairs that can drive any sane person over the edge: the end of the working day is approaching and you have mentally envisioned what you have in your share of the cupboard. In your head, you have put the ingredients together and come up with a genius plan for dinner. By the time you are on your way home, you have virtually tasted the sumptuous dinner you are about to prepare. But in a moment, the crimson mist of "stolen-ingredient rage" is about to descend. You get into the apartment, take off your coat, and kick off your shoes. You put a pan on the range and reach into the cupboard only to grasp at thin air. A noise from the pit of your gut emerges: "*What f*cker has taken my penne?*"

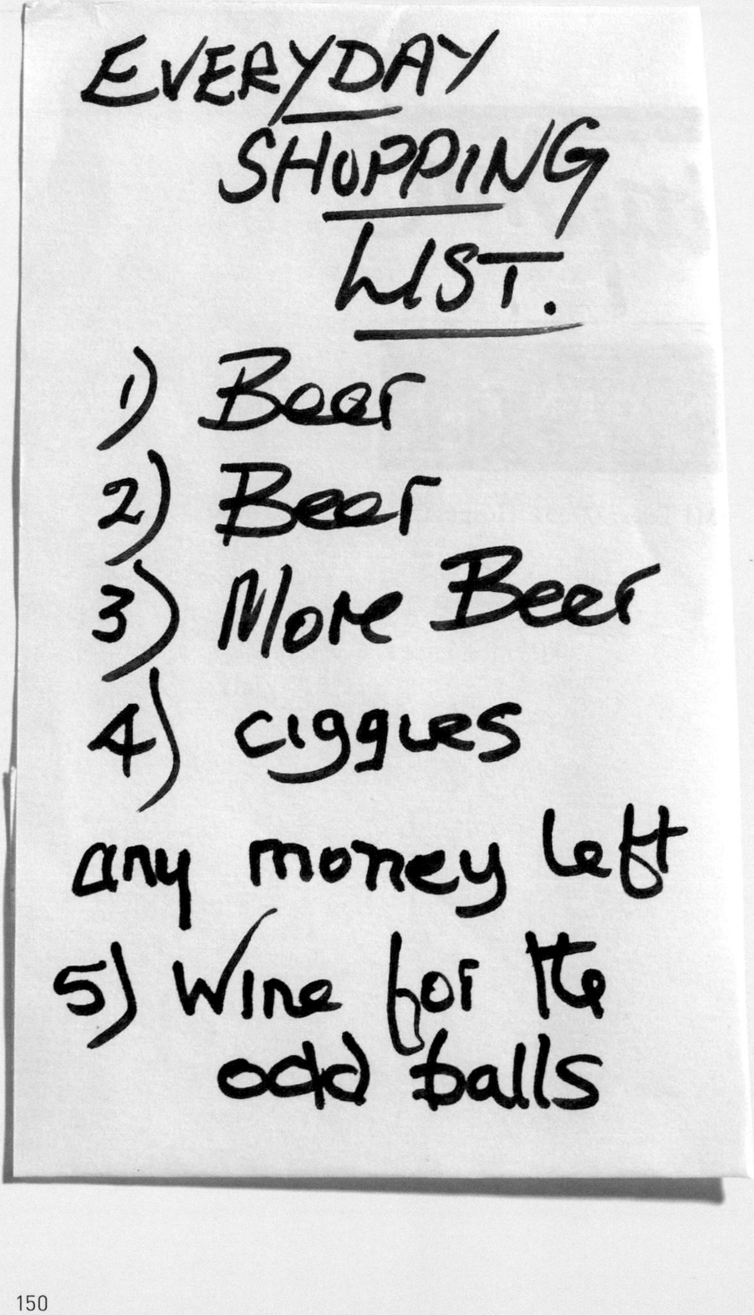
EVERYDAY
SHOPPING
LIST.
1) Beer
2) Beer
3) More Beer
4) ciggies
any money left
5) Wine for the
odd balls

I sometimes think it would be humiliating if people knew what music I had on my iPod. I happily listen to one-hit wonders from the eighties and MOR pop, bobbing along, pretending that I am actually listening to something from a small independent record label that is terribly highbrow and definitely not Wham.

It is for this reason that I like this shopping list. The shopping list I would write down contains lots of words such as "sundried," "mulled" and "organic." The one in my head contains the words "processed," "full fat," and "fun-size." I admire the honesty in this note. All this person really wants is beer and cigarettes, and no other rubbish.

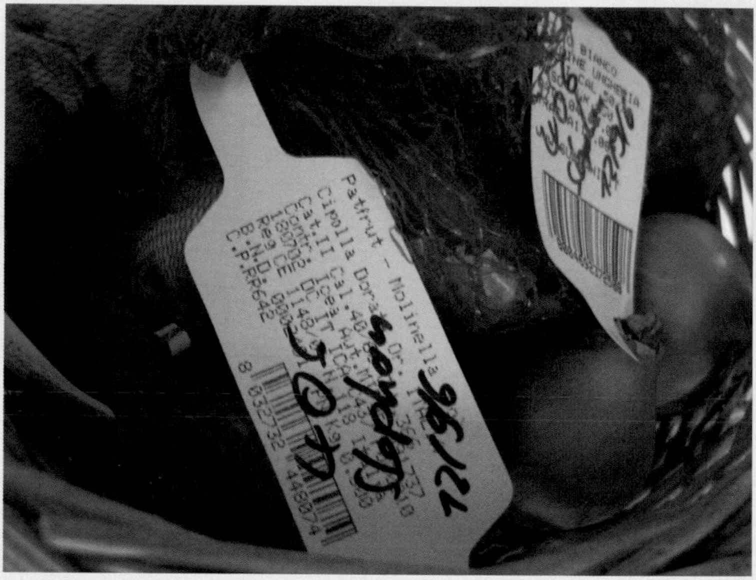
Patfrut - Molinella

In this picture, "Stephen" has put his name on all his onions. Stephen, they are onions. To the best of my knowledge, there is no shortage of onions and in the event you suddenly ran out of them all in one go, unless you live in the Arctic Circle, I do not believe you could not gain access to more onions.

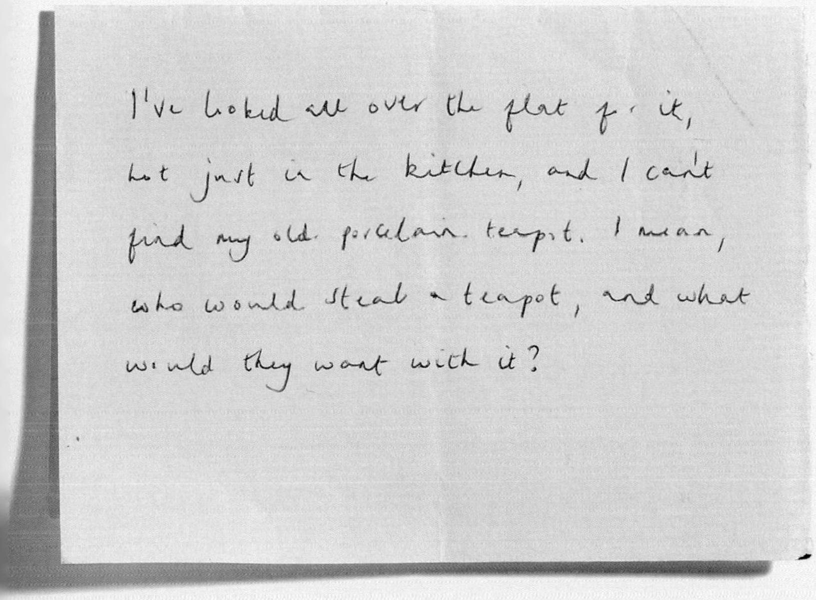

I've looked all over the flat for it, not just in the kitchen, and I can't find my old porcelain teapot. I mean, who would steal a teapot, and what would they want with it?

The sad truth of this note is that nobody stole the teapot—its disappearance was less of a kidnapping than a murder. No theft was involved; this note is about the death of a teapot. Perhaps accidentally nudged off the kitchen table, I suspect the remains were hidden by the culprit under a lot of trash and disposed of quickly, in the hope it would never be mentioned again.

Toaster is hot!
Do not leave plastic on or near appliance;remember to switch button off.
1=on 0=off

Good grief, it sounds like this warning is too late. What horrible accident has happened with plastic near or on the appliance? I am going to have nightmares about molten bread bags wrapping themselves around faces, leaving individuals writhing around their kitchen floors, when all they wanted was a slice of toast for their breakfast.

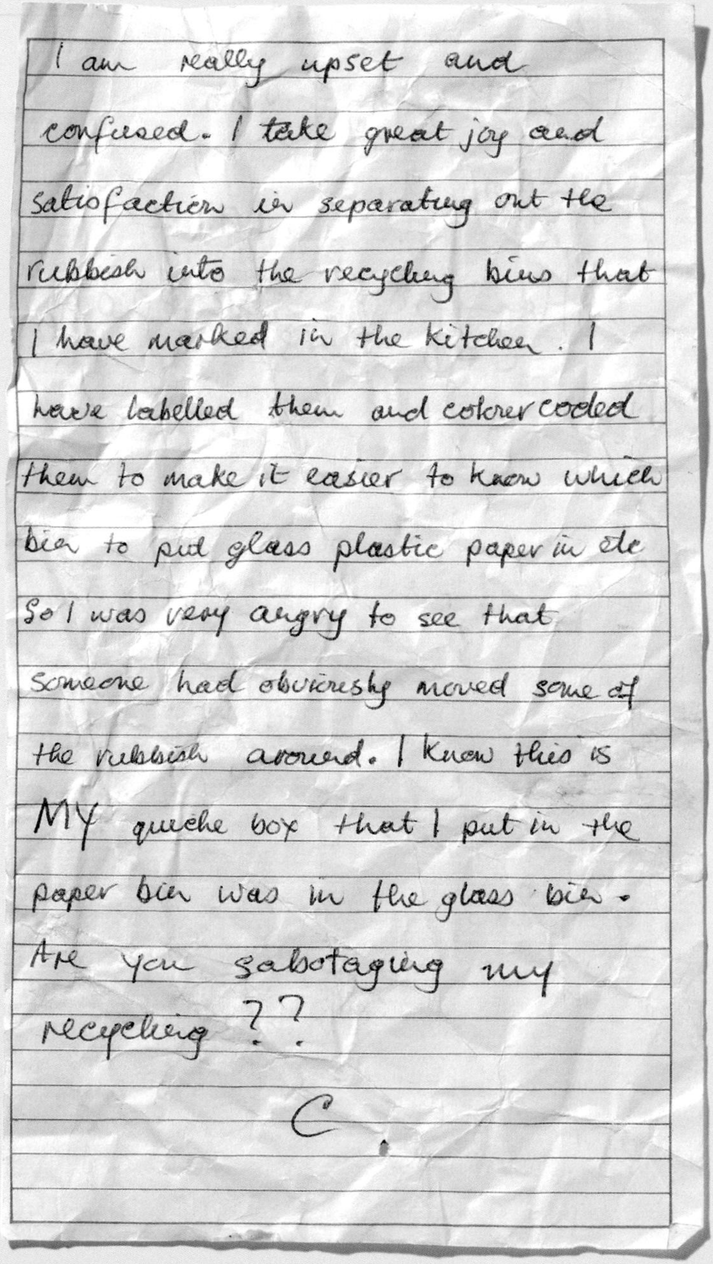

I am really upset and confused. I take great joy and satisfaction in separating out the rubbish into the recycling bins that I have marked in the kitchen. I have labelled them and colour coded them to make it easier to know which bin to put glass plastic paper in etc So I was very angry to see that someone had obviously moved some of the rubbish around. I know this is MY quiche box that I put in the paper bin was in the glass bin. Are you sabotaging my recycling ??

C.

OK, OK, deriving this much joy from recycling sounds a little 70s, but maybe this damn hippie has a point. Green issues have been volleyed about in the political arena for a few decades. Brought up as a last-minute topic—"Oh, by the way the world is heating up and stuff"—they have been treated in the same way as going to the dentist. Everyone knows that they really should go to the dentist regularly, but they always leave it too late, going for an appointment only when an abscess rivaling the size of a human head has appeared. With the environment, the warnings are there; all the aches and pains of the earth are beginning to show, but not until we're all underwater will we really take the issues seriously. Until then, it is lone eco-warriors who will struggle to make the difference against all odds. Although this note makes me want to slap the writer for their quiche-eating, recycling ways, I know they are right.

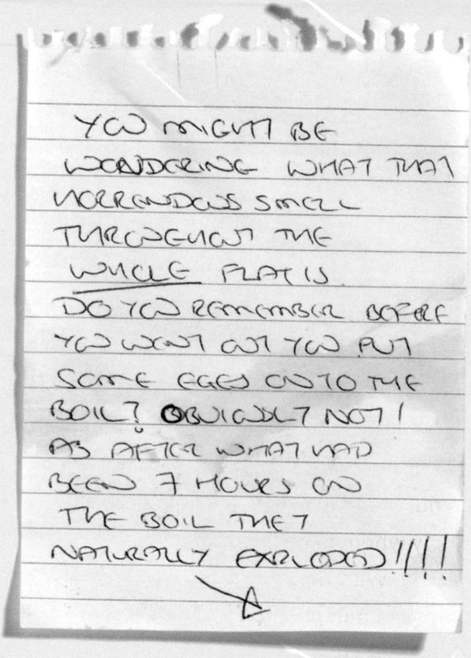

YOU MIGHT BE
WONDERING WHAT THAT
HORRENDOUS SMELL
THROUGHOUT THE
<u>WHOLE</u> FLAT IS.
DO YOU REMEMBER BEFORE
YOU WENT OUT YOU PUT
SOME EGGS ONTO THE
BOIL? OBVIOUSLY NOT!
AS AFTER WHAT HAD
BEEN 7 HOURS ON
THE BOIL THEY
NATURALLY EXPLODED!!!!

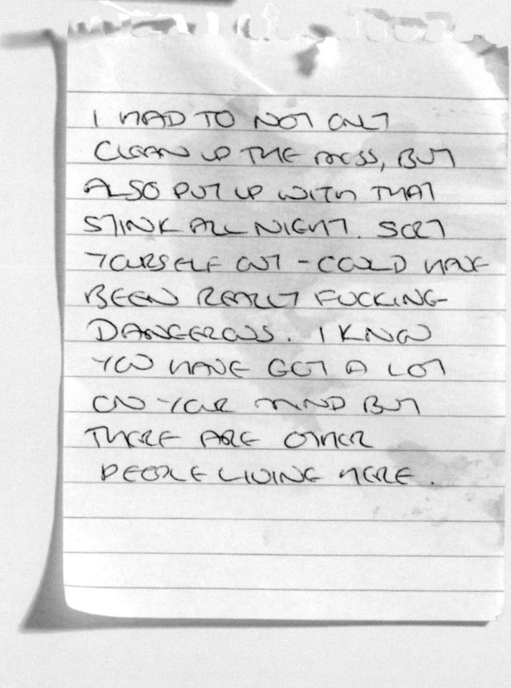

I HAD TO NOT ONLY
CLEAN UP THE MESS, BUT
ALSO PUT UP WITH THAT
STINK ALL NIGHT. SORT
YOURSELF OUT - COULD HAVE
BEEN REALLY FUCKING
DANGEROUS. I KNOW
YOU HAVE GOT A LOT
ON YOUR MIND BUT
THERE ARE OTHER
PEOPLE LIVING HERE.

Eggs can create bad smells. So can burnt-out pans. Exploding, blackened eggs in burnt-out pans raise the bar, however, to a whole new level. What is behind this kind of disaster? If you have a mind full of ideas, some things can easily be categorized as unimportant. As soon as the practical things you should be remembering re-enter your head, they are almost immediately eradicated to make room for the huge, amazing, and monumental new genius thoughts you are growing. I like to think Einstein was always putting eggs on to boil and forgetting about them.

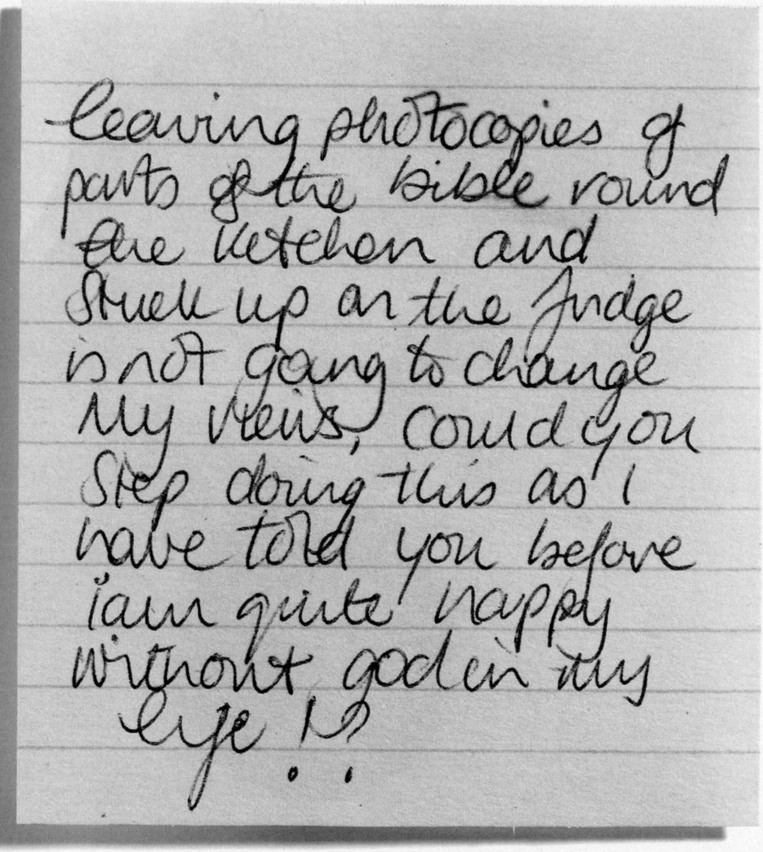

-leaving photocopies of
parts of the bible round
the kitchen and
stuck up on the fridge
is not going to change
my views, could you
stop doing this as i
have told you before
i am quite happy
without god in my
life!!

When the author of this note (we shall call him "Mr. X") moved in, he seemed polite and posh, stating he was only going to be there for a year; the reason being he was engaged and did not want to live with his fiancée before they were married. An unusual decision perhaps, in this day and age, but the roommates were fine with this arrangement. All seemed to be going OK, though Mr. X did seem to talk about the importance of not living in sin a great deal and showed disdain when the other roommates had their partners over to stay the night. The first photocopy of an excerpt from the Bible was treated by the roommates as an oversight by Mr. X—he had simply left out something he was reading or studying. It wasn't until further photocopies started to appear and were finally pinned to the fridge that the roommates realized that Mr. X was on a mission of conversion. Things started to get nasty and apparently came to a head when a discussion about sex before marriage culminated with one of the exasperated roommates asking, "Well, how do you know you're compatible? She might have a weird rubber fetish." Mr. X was apparently very upset at this challenge, let alone the idea of his fiancée being into rubber and, soon after, he moved out. None of the roommates were invited to the wedding.

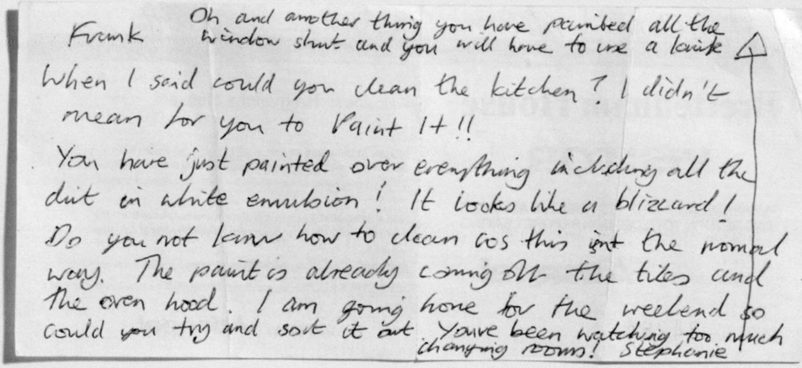
Frank Oh and another thing you have painted all the window shut and you will have to use a knife

When I said could you clean the kitchen? I didn't mean for you to Paint It!!

You have just painted over everything including all the dirt in white emulsion! It looks like a blizzard! Do you not know how to clean cos this isnt the normal way. The paint is already coming off the tiles and the oven hood. I am going home for the weekend so could you try and sort it out. Youve been watching too much changing rooms! Stephanie

I was told in the letter accompanying this note that the issue of cleaning was an argument waiting to happen. After a lot of hints and attempts to cajole Frank into doing some housework, he eventually did it on quite a large scale. Frank described himself as an "all-or-nothing" character and this was the reason he gave for the literal whitewashing of the cleaning. Using some old touch-up paints that had been kicking around their apartment for years, he covered every surface with paint. I am told the kitchen never really got back to normal and every time a cloth was wiped over a surface, white would come off. Stephanie eventually moved out.

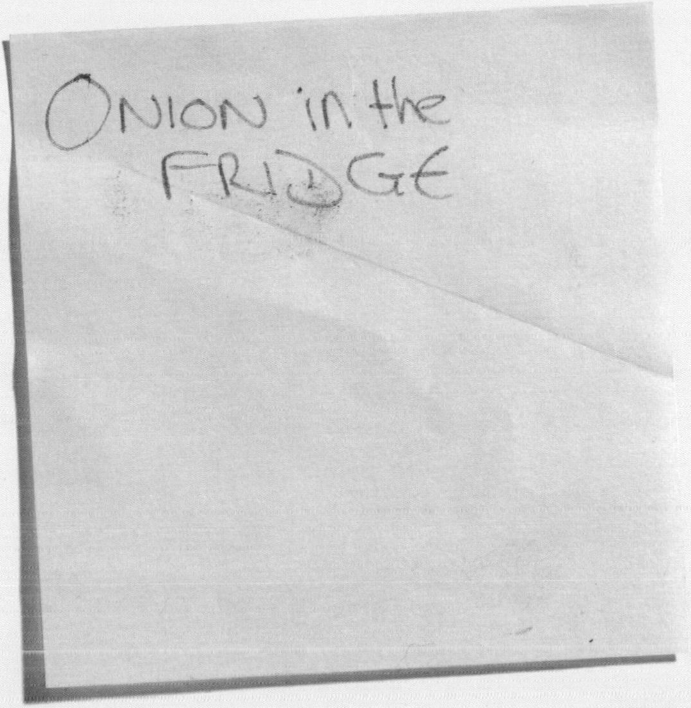
ONION in the FRIDGE

What is it with onions? I did not know they were such a scarce resource or that they were the subject of so much discussion. Or is it a warning, like "sharks in water?" Is there an onion-phobic roommate in the house?

"Why is my bed damp?"

LOVE, SEX, PARTNERS, AND
OTHER NOTES FROM THE BEDROOM

Creativity and the production of new ideas regularly happen in bedrooms. Apart from the most obvious form of creativity that can be performed there (*eeaasssy* now), reading, writing, and, of course, listening to music are mainly done in this room. It is when this creativity seeps out of this room and into the general living space that very creative notes start appearing. The regular thumping noise of what you can only hope is your roommates putting up shelves, but which you fear is something a bit more, well, physical, can ruin a good night's sleep. Equally, being tortured by the thudding of hardhouse techno at 2 A.M. when you are more of a Bob Dylan person can leave you feeling irascible and sleep deprived. The bedroom is meant to be a private space, but is not so in shared accommodation.

You never know what goes on behind closed doors, unless, of course, the doors and walls are paper thin. Living together shatters the illusion of any kind of domestic bliss. You are living out your relationships like a soap opera. This was one of the driving factors behind this book. As a long-suffering space-sharer, I am an experienced voyeur of people's lives. I've watched the ups and the downs, and seen the seemingly perfect often quickly unravel with slams, grunts, and raised voices. To keep up any kind of pretence in the confinements of an apartment is almost impossible, but that doesn't stop most people trying to crack smiles as though they never heard a thing as they pass each other in the hall. For these reasons, sharing a space can be a very good test of a relationship. It bodes well if you can cope with a judge and jury while you are being your most irrational and grumpy, and when your behavior generally leaves a lot to be desired.

However it is also difficult if you are single. Try wooing a new beau when there are not two but three of you squeezed together on the sofa. Or maybe the new squeeze fancies your roommate too and before you know it you are in a sordid three-way relationship, taking one from people you only live with because you need help paying the rent. Terrible.

The bedroom should be a sanctuary—a place to relax and escape your troubles. This is easier said than done, though, when you realize someone else has been relaxing on your bed and left their dirty pants as a fragrant reminder.

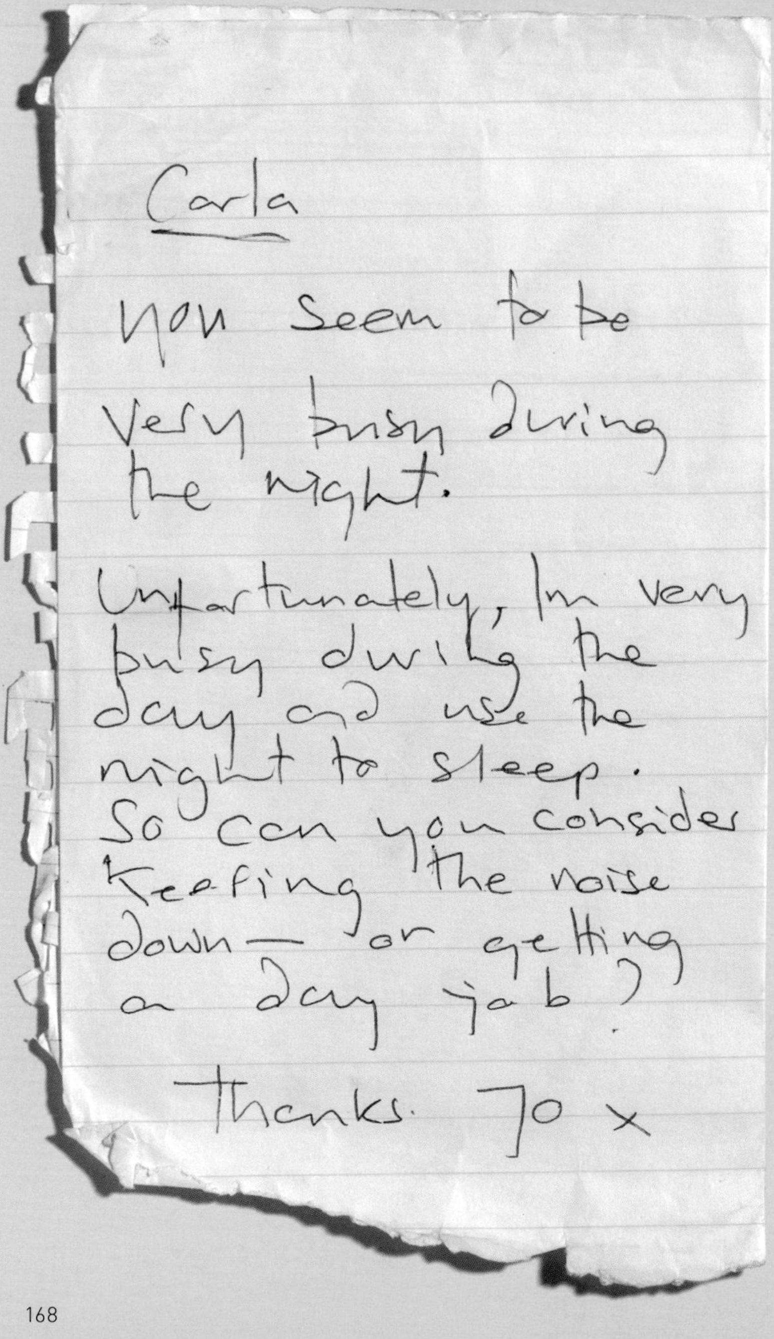

Carla

you seem to be very busy during the night.

Unfortunately, I'm very busy during the day and use the night to sleep. So can you consider keeping the noise down — or getting a day job?

Thanks. Jo x

Some of the notes that have come to me with no explanation are the best. Carla's busy late-night schedule makes the mind boggle.

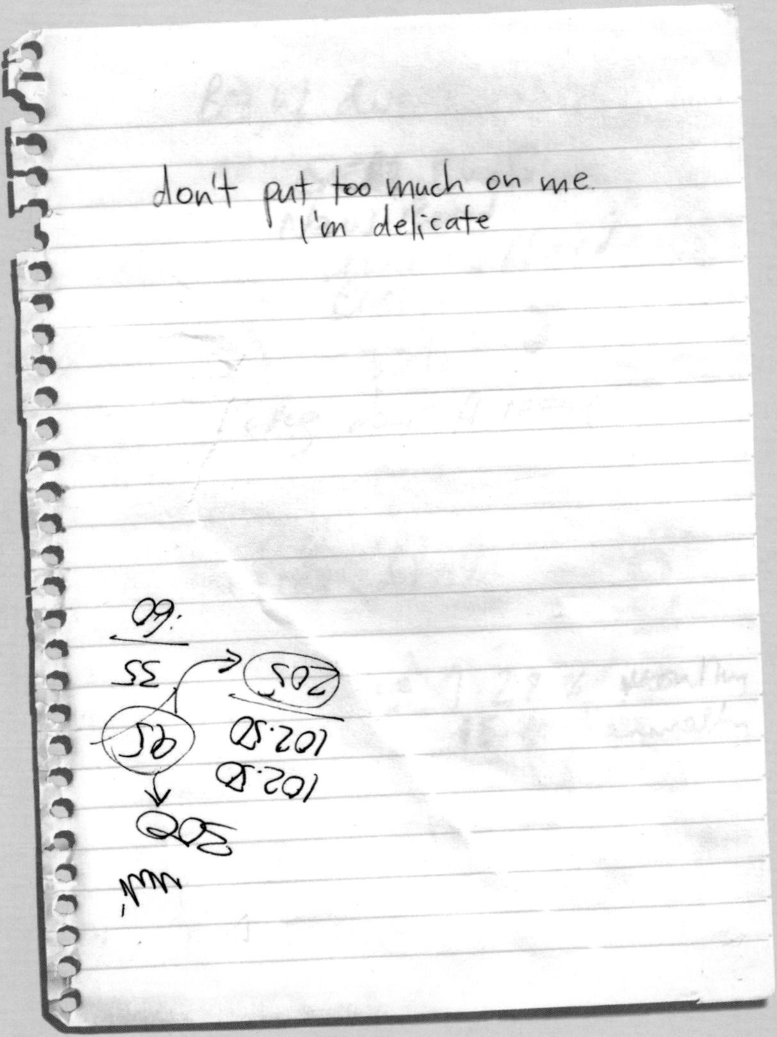

don't put too much on me.
I'm delicate

This is very clever. Effectively you are now rendered utterly mute. Discuss or complain about anything and this person may dissolve into an emotional mess. You might as well cover the floor with eggshells and be done with it. That said, it could be that I am reading far too much into this, for it could be about something much simpler, namely, a table. Though this is possible, it would be a bit fucking weird to start writing notes on behalf of inanimate objects.

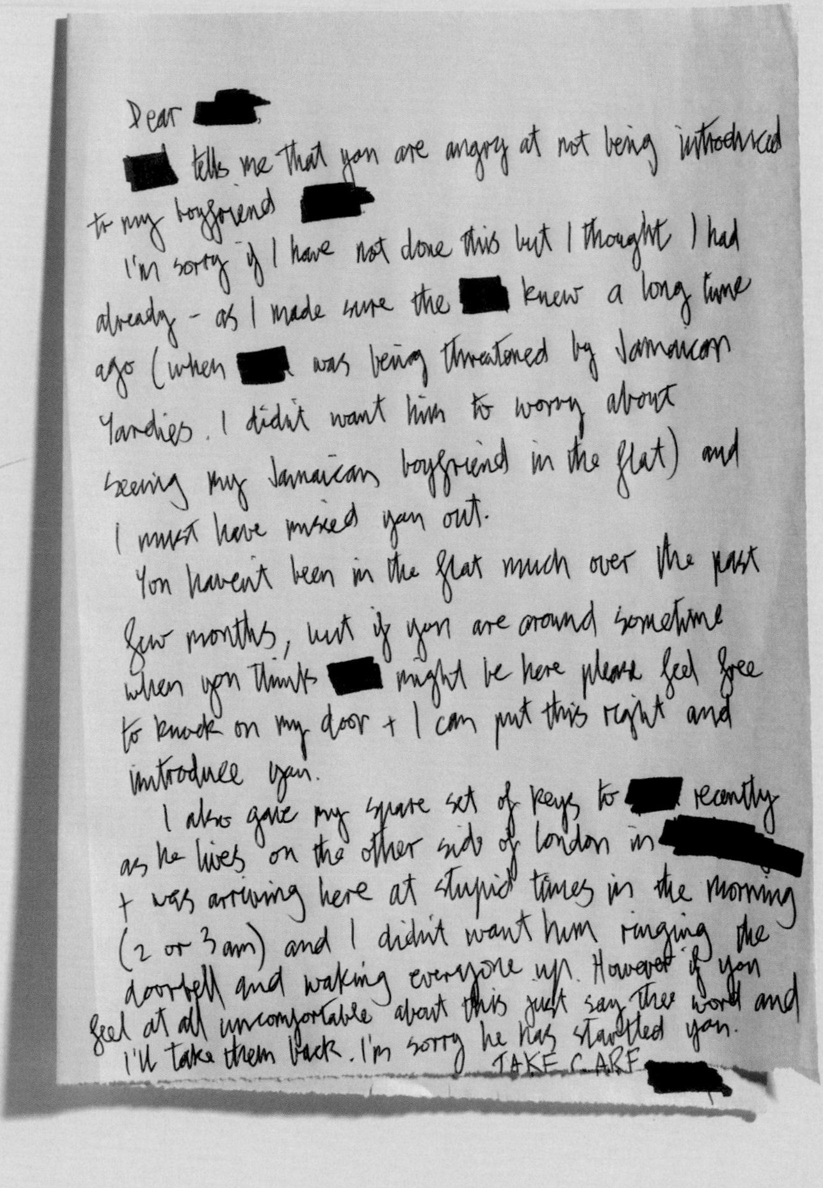

Dear [redacted],

[redacted] tells me that you are angry at not being introduced to my boyfriend [redacted].

I'm sorry if I have not done this but I thought I had already - as I made sure the [redacted] knew a long time ago (when [redacted] was being threatened by Jamaican Yardies. I didn't want him to worry about seeing my Jamaican boyfriend in the flat) and I must have missed you out.

You haven't been in the flat much over the past few months, but if you are around sometime when you think [redacted] might be here please feel free to knock on my door + I can put this right and introduce you.

I also gave my spare set of keys to [redacted] recently as he lives on the other side of London in [redacted] + was arriving here at stupid times in the morning (2 or 3am) and I didn't want him ringing the doorbell and waking everyone up. However if you feel at all uncomfortable about this just say the word and I'll take them back. I'm sorry he has startled you.

TAKE CARE [redacted]

Oh for the love of God, this is complex. So there is a stranger walking around the apartment that you have never met—potentially disconcerting—but this writer seems to have a guilty conscience and has jumped a few steps ahead. The writer seems to be stating her boyfriend is *not* in a gang—did anyone think he was? I am sure they do now after this note. I don't know if this guy should go out with this girl any more because:

a) She seems to presume everyone will think he is a gangster because he is Jamaican.

b) If he is a gangster, she is making everyone very suspicious and doing a good job of blowing his cover.

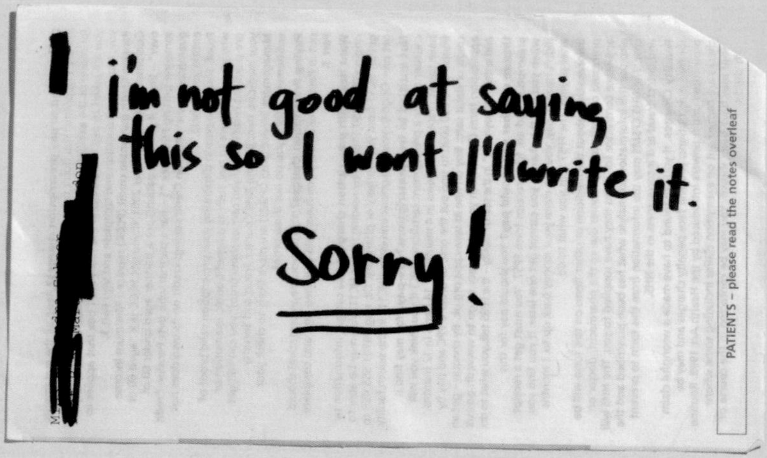
[redacted]
i'm not good at saying this so I wont, I'll write it.
Sorry!
PATIENTS – please read the notes overleaf

This is one of my favorite notes. The main reason is that it is written on the back of a prescription. Not a good sign. This could be the start of a lot of sorry notes. Pass the Valium.

lets make up
forever
X

I am sure this is meant to be a lovely note but I can feel bile gathering in my throat. I bet they even have nicknames for each other. Alternatively it also sounds like a one-sided suggestion for a suicide pact of the "let's spend eternity together" variety. I'm sort of hoping it's the latter scenario.

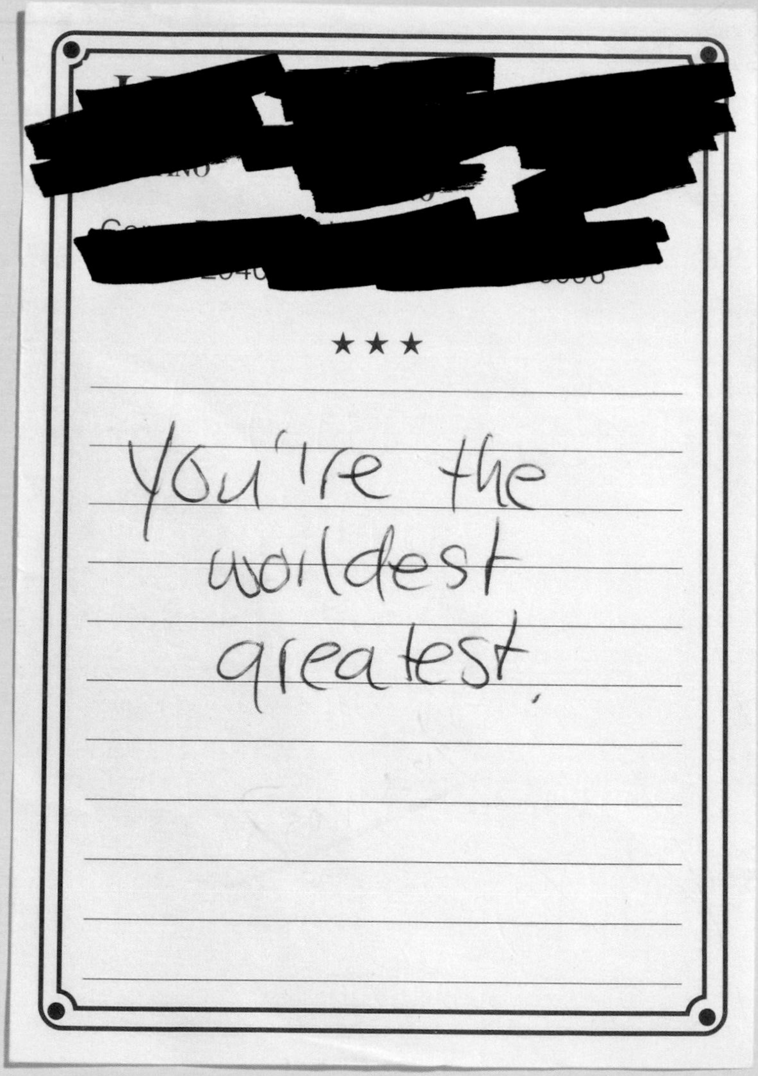
[redacted]
★★★
You're the
worldest
greatest.

To get a note like this is the bestest everest!

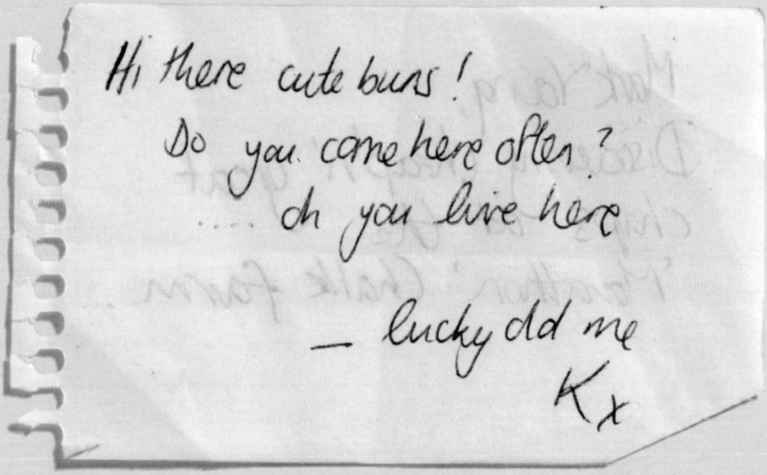
Hi there cute buns!
Do you come here often?
.... oh you live here
— lucky old me
Kx

Roommate flirting can be very good fun, as this note demonstrates, but can also be horrific if you're the one in the middle, not receiving any of the notes. You can be left feeling awkward in your own living space or convinced that as soon as you leave a room there is something going on. There is also the terrible threat of "lucky old me" suddenly deciding "cute buns" isn't so hot anymore—then you feel even more awkward because the only thing happening when you leave the room is a huge argument.

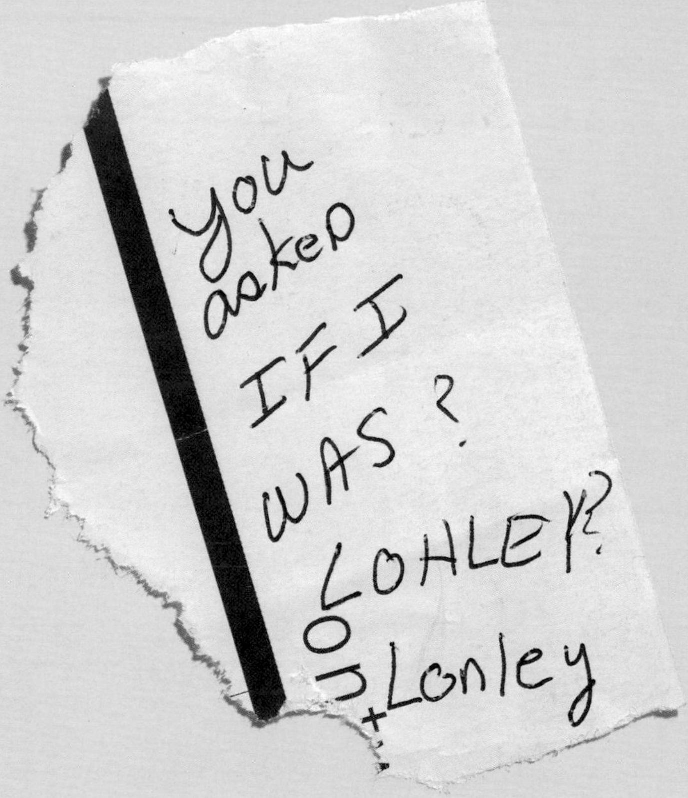
you
asked
IF I
WAS ?
LONLEY?
not
Lonley

you Are
Cute & all

In US
There ARe
LOTS Like
Me

This seems to be a series of love notes, in very broken English, answering some rather creepy questions. Where are there "lots like me?" Why is the writer asking if he or she is lonely? Who is asking these questions? Maybe it's time to call the locksmith.

Now you have seen what
I look in the morning I am
HELEN going to have
to KILL
— x — be stupid you!!
Don't
hun!! xx

A very funny note. It could simply be that Helen was a little dishevelled, panda-eyed, and bedraggled, but I think it is much more entertaining that maybe, just maybe, she was not only bedraggled but starkers! Being caught in the buff by a roommate, or anyone else for that matter, with whom you are not romantically linked, is very embarrassing. It is often made worse by the element of surprise. With no warning, you do not have time to tense muscles and strike a flattering pose. Instead you are generally hopping around putting one leg into underwear, rear aloft, drying toes, or in some other unglamorous position. As you hear the rather shocked viewer scuttling off giggling, you can only wish that you could kill them, wipe their memory, or at the very least pray they believe beauty is not skin deep.

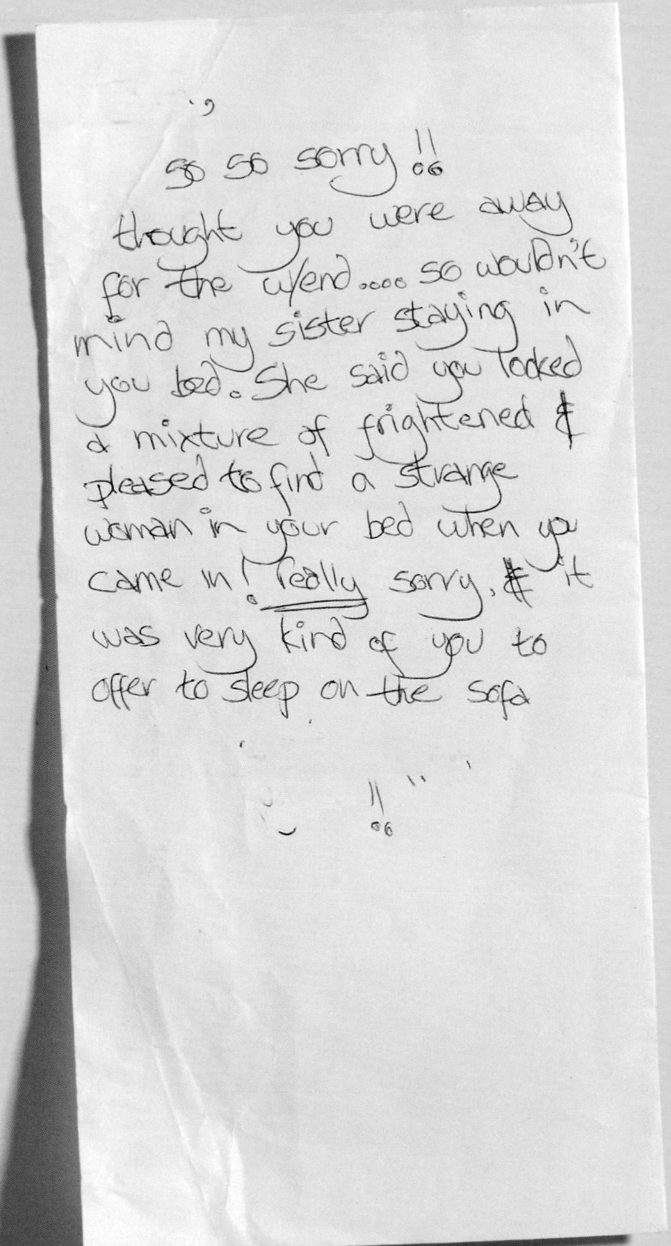

so so sorry!!

thought you were away for the w/end..... so wouldn't mind my sister staying in you bed. She said you looked a mixture of frightened & pleased to find a strange woman in your bed when you came in! really sorry. & it was very kind of you to offer to sleep on the sofa

!!

The young gentleman in this note didn't know if his Christmases had all come at once, or if he should call the police. He arrived home very late to find a young lady safely tucked up in his bed in her underwear. Both were equally shocked to see each other and there then followed some very awkward, quick explanations and apologies. The young lady then exited the bed to sleep in the living room. She was not the result of our gentleman rubbing a lamp, but the visiting sister of his roommate. Now nicknamed "Goldilocks," she opted not to stay again but to get the night bus home before she got a reputation.

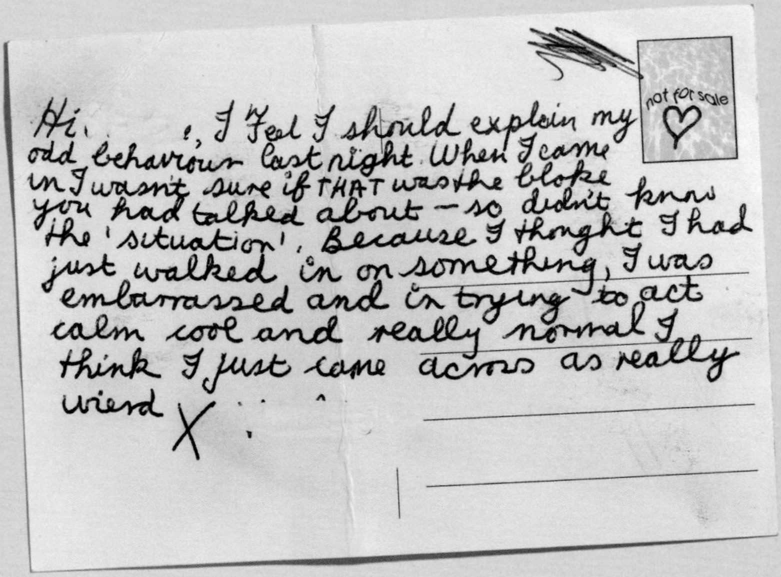
Hi , I Feel I should explain my
odd behaviour last night. When I came
in I wasn't sure if THAT was the bloke
you had talked about – so didn't know
the 'situation'. Because I thought I had
just walked in on something, I was
embarrassed and in trying to act
calm cool and really normal I
think I just came across as really
wierd X

not for sale

Whether you like it or not, you tend to know more than you would like to about people that you live with. This is especially odd as they might not necessarily be people you would have chosen to be friends with. This poor soul has come home from a day at work and suddenly had to work out all sorts of unspoken dynamics. It can be very difficult to pick up on subtle emotional nuances and, in your desperation not to put the proverbial foot in it, you can come across as cold, enigmatic, or worse, just plain stupid. Suddenly when asked simple questions, you have no idea how to answer. "Do you live here?" "I don't know, do I?"

WHY
IS
MY
BED
DAMP?

I pray that this was simply a matter of a window being left open, or that a helpful roommate had washed the bedding and it was still slightly moist. Yet I can't help thinking there is something much, much darker behind this note.

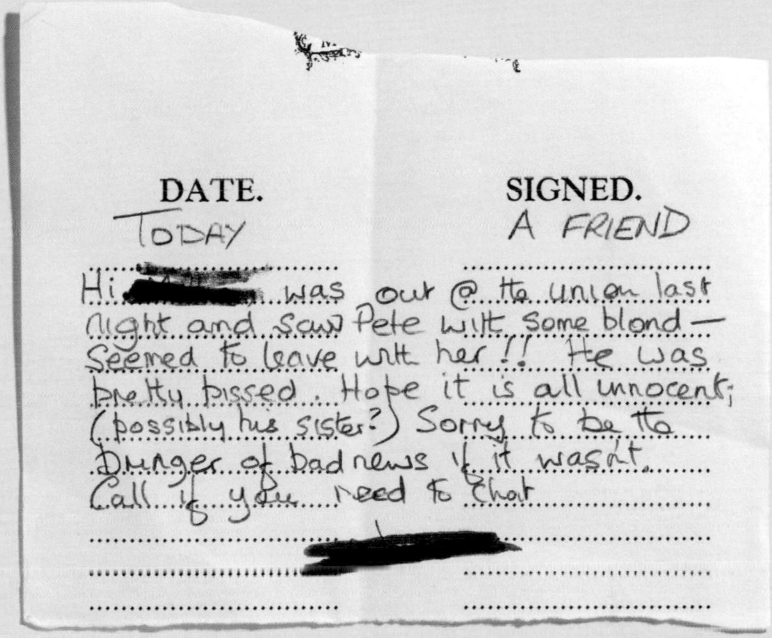

DATE. SIGNED.

TODAY A FRIEND

Hi [redacted] was out @ the union last night and saw Pete with some blond — Seemed to leave with her!! He was pretty pissed. Hope it is all innocent; (possibly his sister?) Sorry to be the bringer of bad news if it wasn't. Call if you need to chat

[redacted]

It's hard not to suspect that there are some people who enjoy being the bringer of bad tidings. They always seem to know everyone's business and are in the center of every drama. Their sentences often start with "I don't want to be a gossip" or "I'm not being a bitch," before swiftly turning to something bitchy or scandalous. Faux confidants are dangerous people. When they ask you how you are or how you feel, with a helpful arm around you, they are working out the quickest way to report your demise to every corner of the world.

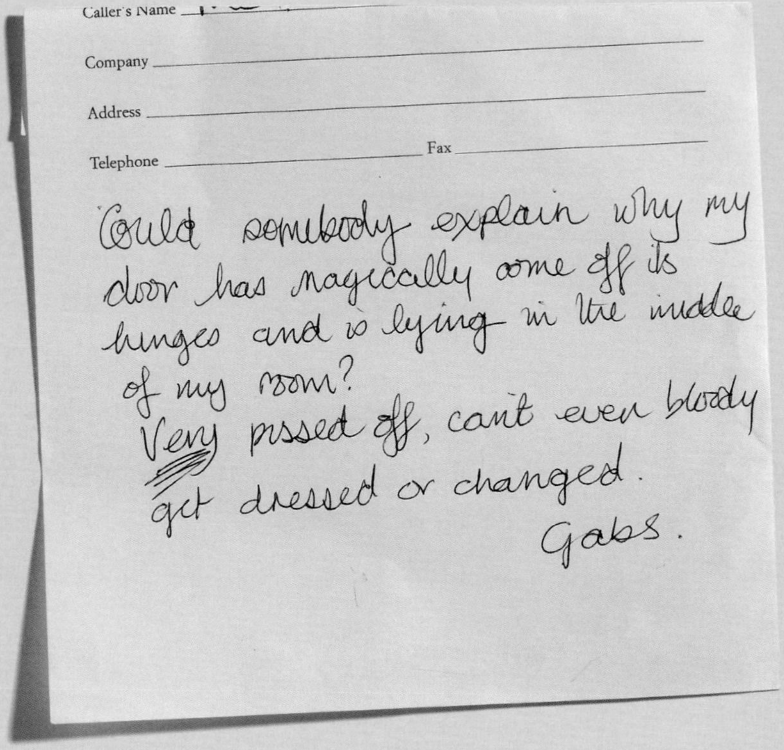
Caller's Name

Company

Address

Telephone Fax

Could somebody explain why my door has magically come off its hinges and is lying in the middle of my room?
Very pissed off, can't even bloody get dressed or changed.
Gabs.

When this note was passed to me, it was obvious the writer was still "very pissed off." I began to understand her emotional state when she elaborated further. The door had been a bit on the wobbly side, as it was an old place with old doors. She suspected a roommate had pushed at it to get into her room and borrow her hairdryer, and had used such force that the door, which was not very stable in the first place, came right off its hinges and hey, *timber*! Things were made worse by the fact it was very heavy and, en route to the floor, put a huge dent in her table and smashed some small ornaments to obliteration. Nice.

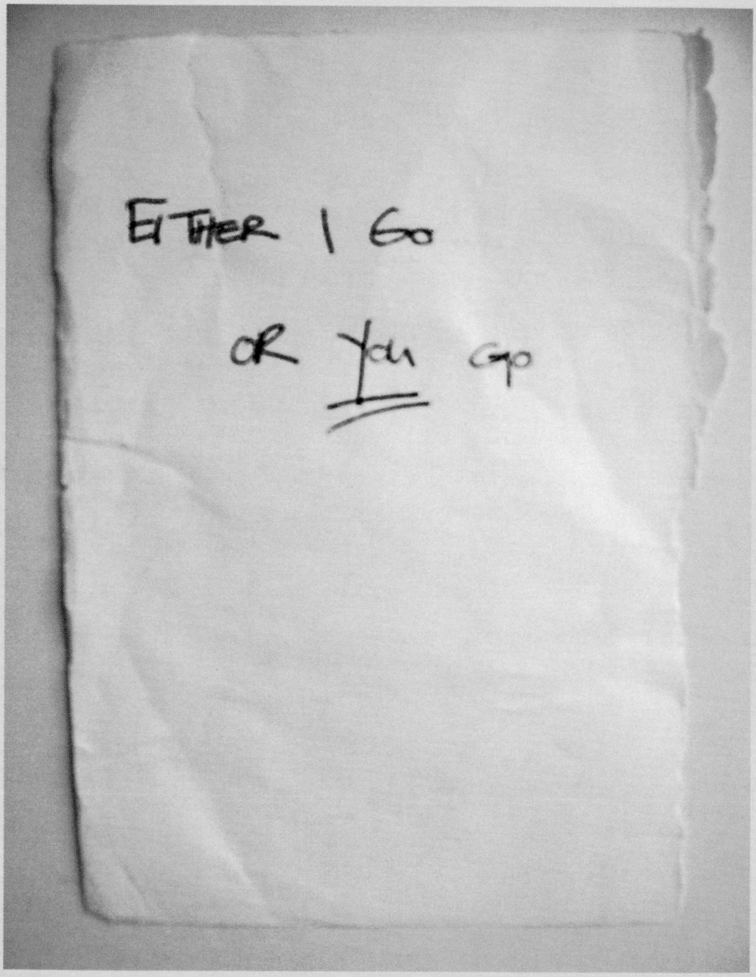
EITHER I GO
OR YOU GO

I am guessing that this note is not quite as it seems. I am basing this presumption on a roommate story I was told involving a cute cat. My friend said that he moved in with a group of friends and their very lovely kitten. Things were good at first, but very quickly the sneezing and itching started. Yes, my friend was allergic to the cat. My friend said that it got to the point where, like in this note, it became obvious that they could not live together and one of them had to go. Somewhat inevitably, it was my friend who became the stray and had to find allergy-free accommodation. Thus I hope this note is about someone who is allergic to dumb dogs. I know I find it hard to stay in the same room as a stupid bitch.

I HATE YOU
MORE THAN
LIFE ITSELF

What the hell did the recipient do to deserve this note? Or were they completely innocent? When I study this note closely, it looks as though it has been stuck to a wall or door and not just left on a table. Hmm. Determined. In these kinds of scenarios, it's probably best to just have a large supply of "sorry" notes to distribute, because trying to work out what the problem is could just push this note writer over the edge.

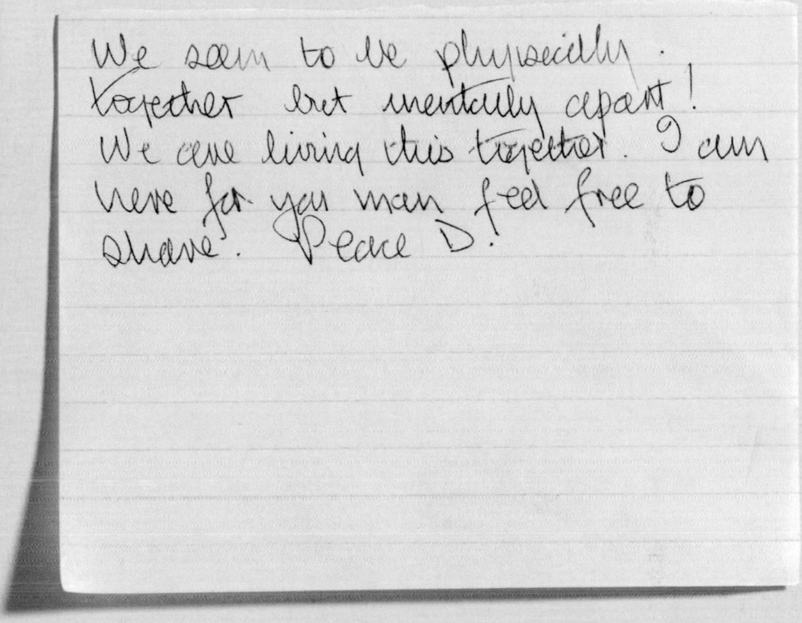
We seem to be physically.
together but mentally apart!
We are living this together. I am
here for you man feel free to
share. Peace D!

Amazingly this note was written in the twenty-first century and not on the back of an acid tab in 1973. Peace.

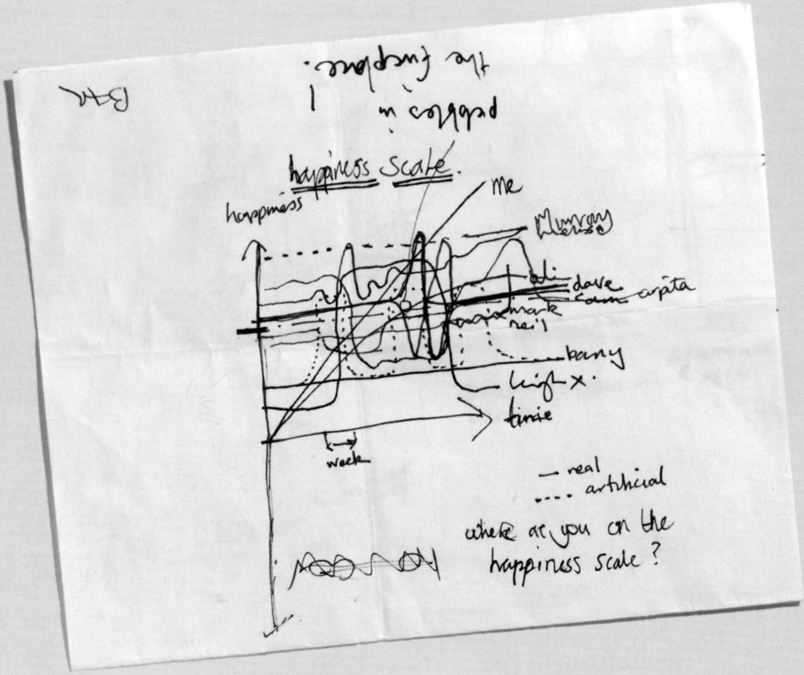
happiness scale.
happiness
me
dave
neil
barry
time
week
— real
---- artificial
where are you on the
happiness scale?

Sitting down and actually working out your levels of happiness can be very therapeutic and revealing. Are you happier, happiest, or hoping to be happy? On this graph, some are off the scale while others are still in the negative numbers. This is one of the most creative submissions and one I look forward to seeing in psychiatric textbooks in years to come.

HOSTILE COMMUNICATION

SUN 20 — MARCH

TAT

ARNE

SUN 2/4/06

HOUSE MEETING Postponed!

8-15.

DONT BE LATE.

ON LOVE ISLAND (ie BED)

I have met these two and they are a lovely couple who live together. They have devised a system that I think all couples should use: a "nice scale." It is a visual tool to show when either of them have been, well, a tool. Every harsh word or unreasonable action is represented by a black mark against the inflictor's name. Looking closely at this picture, I think Arne is due to buy Iat some flowers very soon. I am not quite sure if there were any actual penalties incurred if you got a certain amount of "not nice" points, but I would have thought that the fact you could see it on a board would be enough to make you change your ways. There is also the question of what amounts to "not nice" and this again depends on a person's standards. I was once questioned by one of my prolific note-writing roommates as to what it would take before I wrote a note to her. I thought about it for some time before saying if she peed on the floor that might upset me. Unfortunately, this concept and my rather crass turn of phrase made her write a long note about the conversation. It was a real no-win situation. She was sensitive, I was not. I'm sure my "not nice" column would have been maxed out.

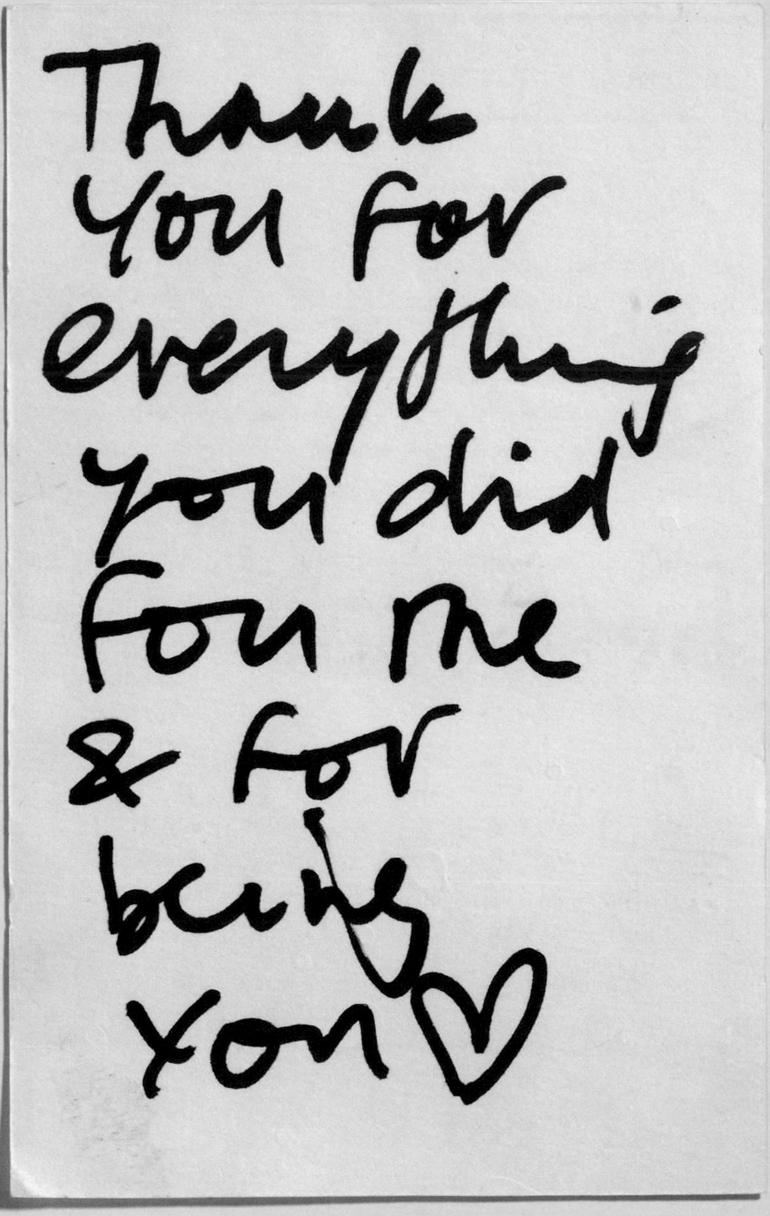
Thank you for everything you did for me & for being you ♡

Have you ever thought that if you dropped down dead not only would nobody notice but also you would probably be stepped over? No one cares so you won't care. This can lead to a grim outlook on mankind. This is when you get your elbows out when shopping, don't give change to street musicians (and sometimes even kick their dog), and positively hate anyone who cracks a smile. There are times when you just want to curl up under a duvet with a Valium, or sit on the sofa scoffing at losers on reality TV. It is just at these points in your life when you hate yourself and everyone around you that a note like this can mean the world. The cynic in me wants to make all sorts of retching noises and talk about the nausealing sweetness of this note, but it is too easy to mock. Fact is, I'd like to think it wasn't easy to write it. In any event, as a recipient it's good to think that not only have you done something kind and not had it thrown back in your face, but you have done something kind that didn't put you through hell and back—you just had to be yourself. A "thank you" or a "love you," or a note like this is enough to make you emerge blinking like Gollum from out of the bedclothes, put down the barbiturates, turn off Simon Cowell, shave, and start viewing life a bit more positively. We all have duvet days and the fact that you managed to help someone out of their depression should help you out of yours. I think if someone gave me this note, I would keep it in my pocket, so when a shopper had just elbowed me and all felt hopeless, I would remember that it was OK just being me.

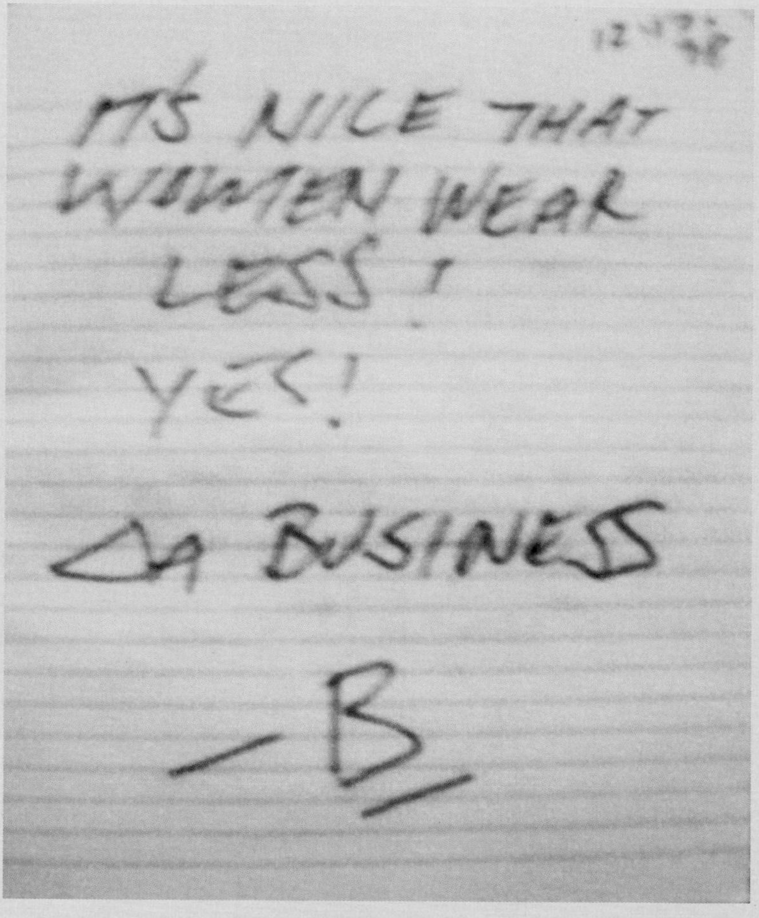
ITS NICE THAT
WOMEN WEAR
LESS!
YES!
A BUSINESS
B

That someone was compelled to write this note is almost touching. What vision, what demi-goddess did he see that inspired a public announcement once they got home? And wear less—less than what? Before? "Da business" doesn't sound like it comes from someone who has just arrived from a land where women are covered head to toe. Or maybe this person has gone through a late puberty—the scales have just dropped from his eyes and he's suddenly acutely aware of every curve on every female.

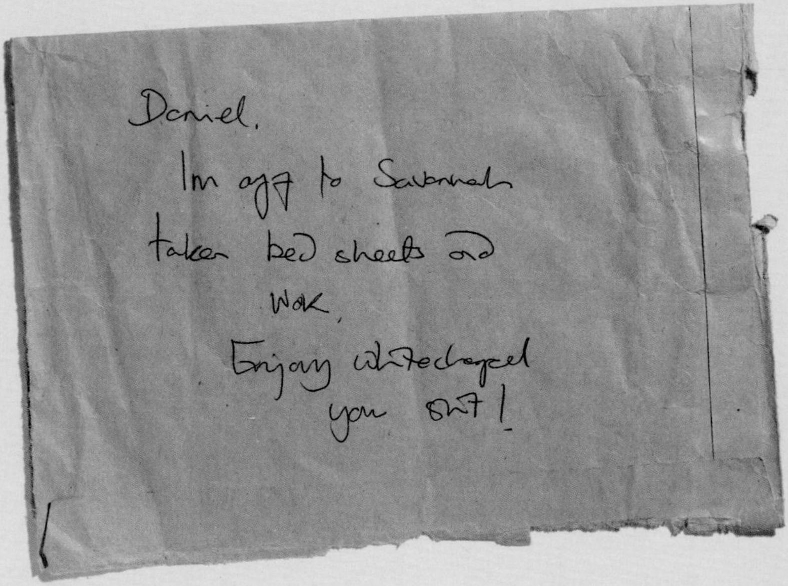
Daniel,
Im off to Savannah
taken bed sheets and
wok,
Enjoy Whitechapel
you shit!

In the end, I hear this couple went to Savannah together, where I am happy to say they are still sharing their wok.

Dear [redacted]

Our phone bill has been very large since you moved in. I don't think we should split it as I have noticed in the itemising a lot of 0898 numbers being called at night and I dont think we should pay for your expensive "hobbie"!!

[redacted]

It's a bit weird when you find out someone you know is a bit of a perv. It goes into the same category as finding out that someone you think is really cool and interesting likes wine bars and Celine Dion.

Being a perv is OK if you make it apparent from the start—you know, gimp-masked up, rubber pants, and asking to be whipped—but being caught off guard can be really confusing. When a friend of mine went to get her nose pierced, a guy in a very sensible suit came in, ripped open his shirt and tie, and got his nipples pierced. Again, that's just confusing. If I go to the post office, I don't want to start wondering if the old lady behind the desk is actually wearing anything below that desk. In any case, this sex-line caller doesn't sound like a perv, just bored. I think he actually gets turned on by these notes. He probably doesn't even listen to the dirty dialogue because he's too busy getting off on the letters from this angry lady.

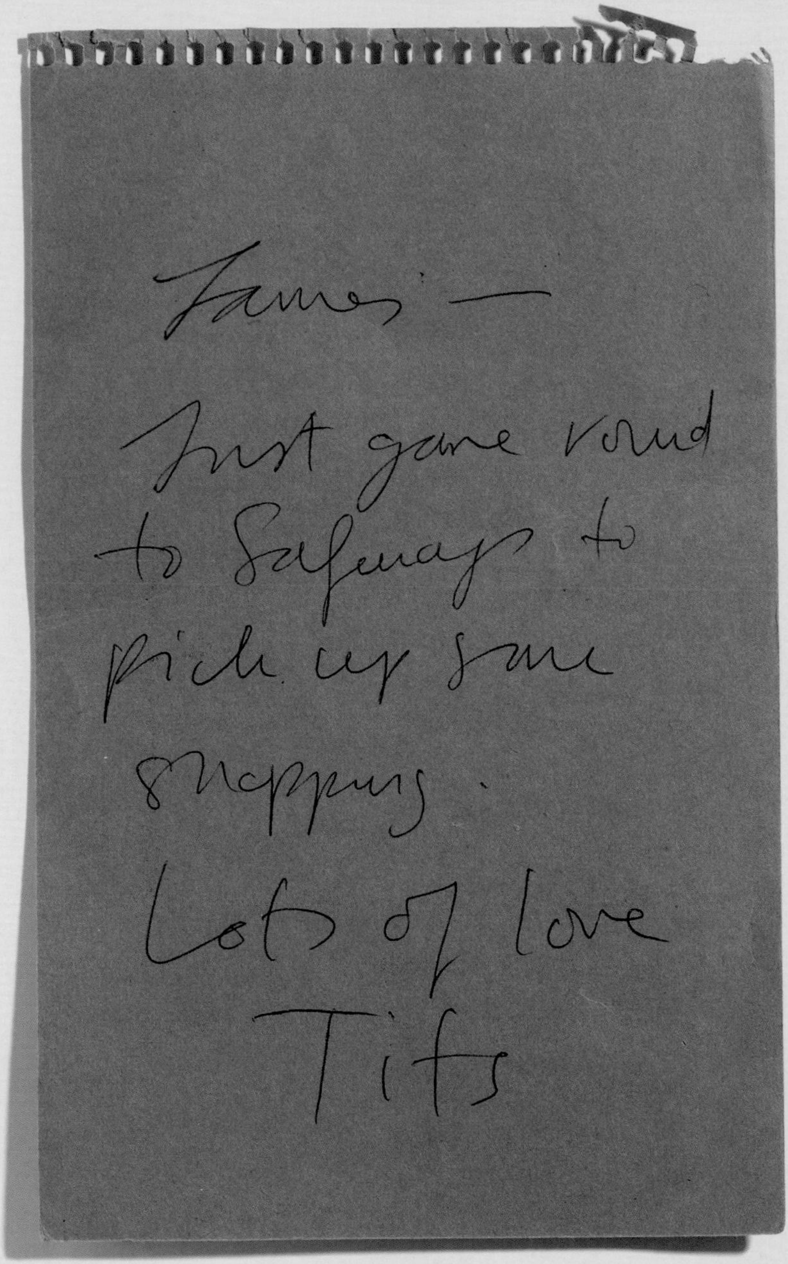
James —

Just gone round to Safeways to pick up some shopping.

Lots of love

Tifs

Who on earth is called Tits? And more to the point, who refers to *themselves* as Tits? Is this one of those weird girls you can hire to do the housework? I didn't know they would go to the shops naked. Surely that's just dangerous. Never mind the swerving oncoming traffic, think of the chafing from the seatbelt on poor Tits. Hold on, have I misread this? Are they going shopping for "love tits?" What are love tits? Where can you buy these love tits? Maybe they are simply those sidesplitting, breast-shaped chocolates you can buy at the back of card shops in empty shopping malls. Unfortunately I know the background to this one. For better or worse, nobody is buying any special chocolates or sex toys. Anita, whose nickname is "Tita," wrote the note. Amusingly, when it's written in a rush on the way to going to the shops, the "a" looks distinctly like an "s," and suddenly Tita is Tits. Before you ask, yes, Tita has got a big chest.

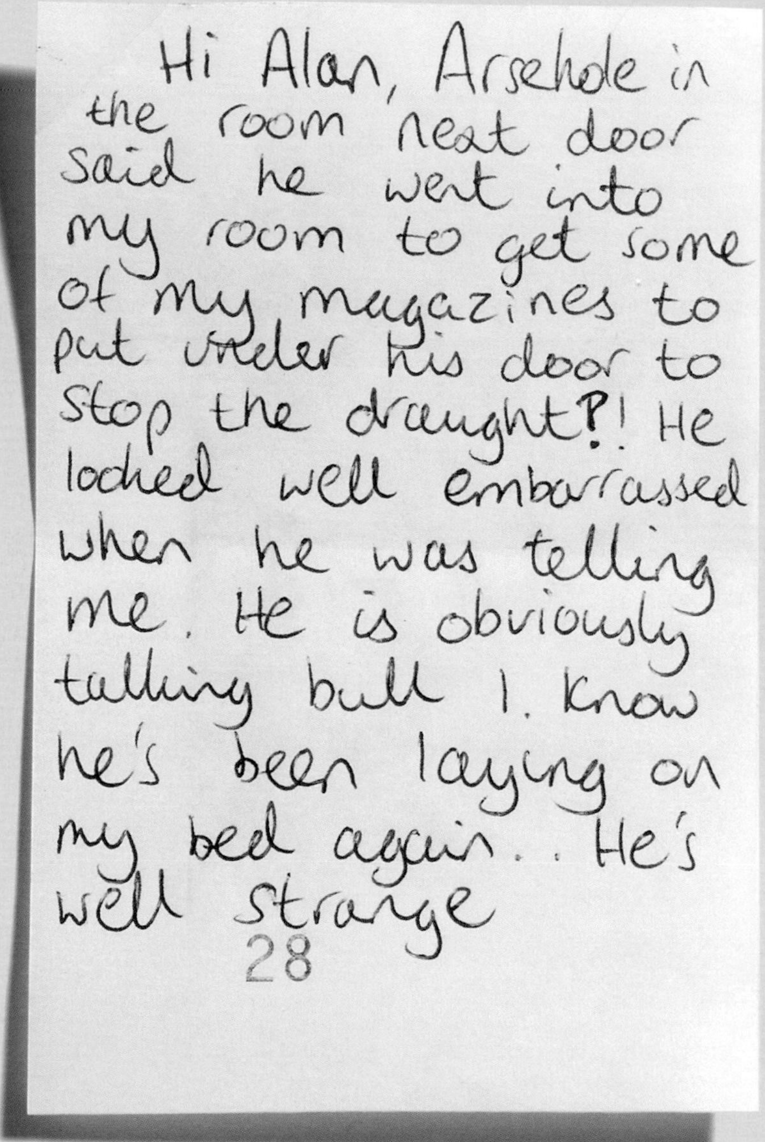
Hi Alan, Arsehole in the room next door said he went into my room to get some of my magazines to put under his door to stop the draught?! He looked well embarrassed when he was telling me. He is obviously talking bull I. Know he's been laying on my bed again.. He's well strange

28

This note is awful on so many levels. It starts with a truly baffling excuse that must have taken some time to digest and understand as it is obviously a lie. The fact that "arsehole" is lying on the bed *again* is the terrifying bit and that elaborate explanations are being constructed to cover it up. This makes you think he is not innocently reading on the bed. The next worry is does he secretly want you to know that he lies on your bed? "Strange" is the biggest understatement about this individual.

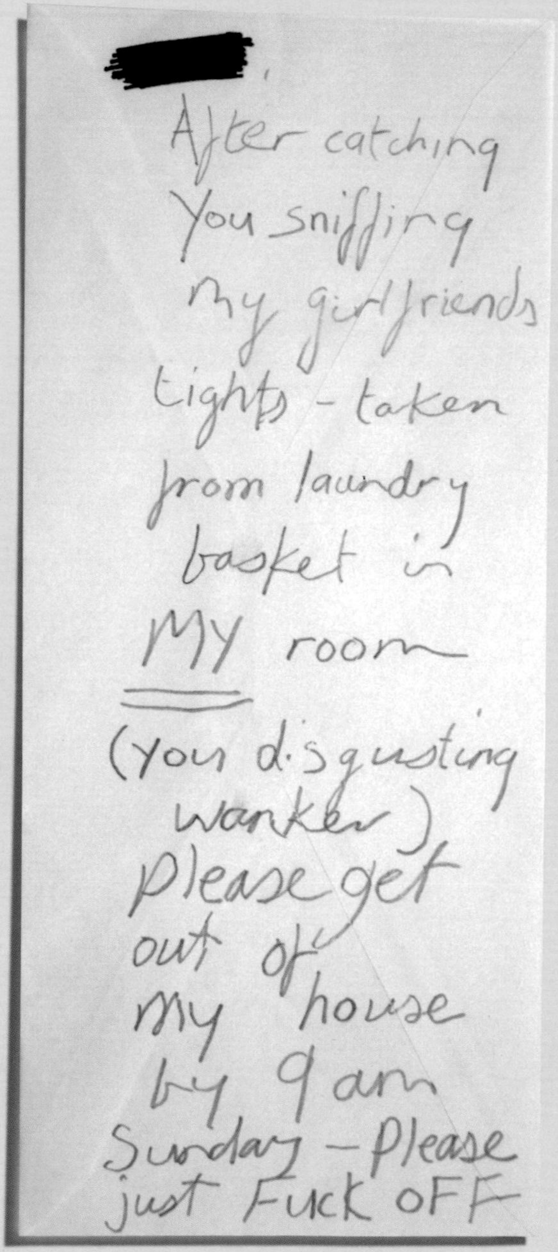

[redacted],

After catching
You sniffing
my girlfriends
tights - taken
from laundry
basket in
MY room
(You disgusting
wanker)
Please get
out of
my house
by 9 am
Sunday - Please
just FUCK OFF

"Catching" and "sniffing" are two words you don't want to see in the same sentence, especially in reference to your girlfriend's tights. I wonder if it was the crotch or the feet area of the tights that were being sniffed. Or was the violator a bit of a refined connoisseur and went along the whole length of the leg like a fine Cuban cigar?

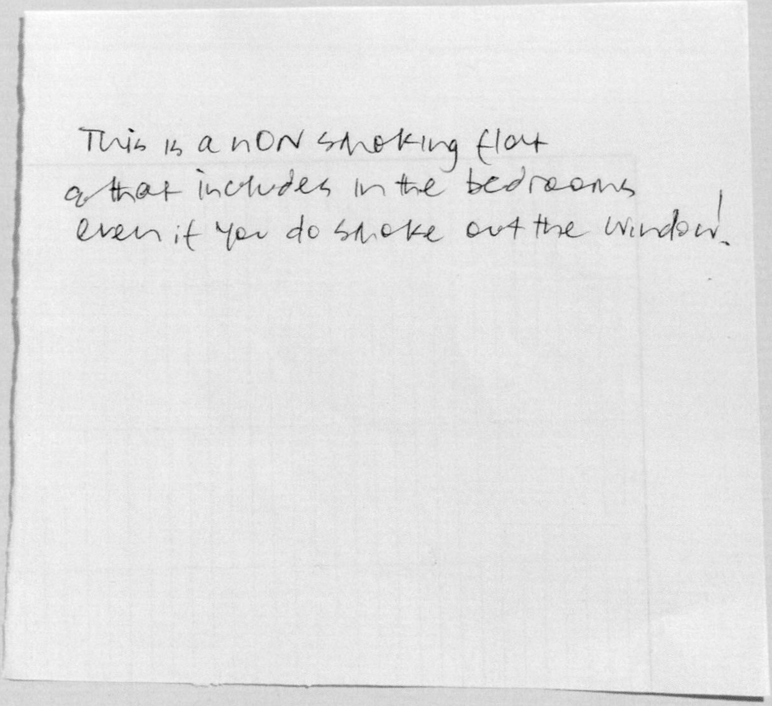
This is a NON smoking flat
a that includes in the bedrooms
even if you do smoke out the window!

I think it is only a matter of time before I write a book about apartment deaths. We have had eggs exploding, plastic melting, and, potentially, people falling out of windows having a secret cigarette. It is true that smoking may kill you, but just quicker than you think if you keep hanging out of windows.

Laura dear
thankyou for being lovely —
I'm such a TWAT.
xxx

No explanation needed.

Afterword

This book may be coming to a conclusion, but the trials and tribulations of living with others are neverending while you're renting. We are the little people: the people who don't buy *House and Garden* magazine because we don't have either; the people who have been saved from the hell of Ikea as the place we live in is not ours to decorate. We are the renters—the ones stuck in limbo with no property ladder to hang on to. That said, the security of owning your own place often takes away the chance of sharing with a bunch of randoms. And whichever way you look at it, sharing your space with others makes you stronger and more interesting whether you like it or not.

We humans seem to be unsure whether we are better off as individual creatures who are meant to have their own little cave to shuffle around in or as pack animals wanting to groom, eat, and generally hang out together. The Internet reflects this ambiguity. You can guarantee those who are keenest on making virtual friends have distinctly fewer friends in the real world. Yes, the *real* world.

The best bit about compiling this book has been the people I have met or talked about. You can't help feeling you know or have met someone similar when you read the notes. Sometimes, just sometimes, you cringe as you recognize yourself. C'mon, admit it. The book has forced me to look at my own weird habits, and though I don't have obsessive-compulsive disorder, I do have "a friend" who can't go to bed if they think the ornaments in the living room are not lined up straight. OK, that's right, the straight ornaments will make everything better.

If you have taken to eating your dinner in the locked bathroom to avoid social interaction in your apartment, then this may be the perfect tactful gift for the nemesis you have ended up living with. Just leave the book on their bed, open at the relevant page. Unlike most communication today, the notes are mainly written by hand (as opposed to typed). The choice of paper and the writing provide ample material for analysis, and for that reason the book has become almost like a counseling session. It can be cathartic to find out there are people in more fucked-up situations than you. Take solace from the book. Sit back and ponder why some of these people live together or how some of them manage to live at all.

On the other hand, if you have got to the end of this book and felt that you have notes that make these pale into insignificance, you still have an opportunity to let the world know by adding your notes to the Web site (www.roommatesanonymous.com). Surely that would be the sweetest revenge of all. Not only that, but if you visit the Web site you might meet people that you actually like. Along with adding or viewing notes, you could also get some advice on your own roommate situation. And, if all else fails, you could try advertising for a new roommate on the site. You might find the perfect match. For example: Wanted, a roommate who doesn't leave crusty underwear in the bathroom, but just cleans it. Yes, find a new roommate from the Web site—at least you know you like reading the same books.

To conclude, during my research I came across several university sites offering help and guidance on living together. My favorite was run by the Swinburne College Australia (www.swinburne.edu.au).

To quote the site:

> *How to share successfully:*
>
> *In order to make sharing a success, you need to establish your house rules with those with whom you will be sharing. Some important considerations when seeking shared accommodation are:*
>
> - *cost*
> - *number of people in the household and their ages*
> - *male/female ratio*
> - *proximity to campus and public transport*
> - *special dietary requirements such as vegetarianism*
> - *smokers to non-smokers in the household*
> - *cultural differences*
> - *common interests of those in the household*

Great advice, except not all of us are sensible, mature, rational, and selfless individuals. With the best will in the world, living with others will always have its ups and downs, but it is preferable to living as a hermit, growing long fingernails, and weeing in bottles. How boring life would be if you did follow these rules, and how little you would appreciate your own space if you always had it.

Acknowledgments

Just before I sign off to set up my own virtual apartment, eat virtual pies, and watch virtual porn with virtually no mates, there are a few people I would like to thank.

Thank you to family and friends, but more so to foes. The foes gave me the impetus to get this book underway and exorcise their demons from my memory. Thank you to many of my students for their input. Thank you Alan D, who I would always be happy to live with again. Big, big thank you to Adelaide for generally lots of things and helping with the book—I miss finding you milling around the living room. Extremely large and neverending thank you to Mr. M. Young—my favorite "flatmate" in the world. Thank you to Gordon Wise and to everyone at Little Brown, especially Antonia Hodgson. Also, a huge thank you to David Cashion and everyone at Abrams Image for all their hard work and for having faith in an eccentric Brit.

CAT POO!